Arts: A Second Level Course

Renaissance and Reformation   Units 7–14

Florence

Unit 8   Sculpture 1400–1470

Unit 9   Architecture: Brunelleschi and Alberti 1400–1472

Unit 10   Painting 1300–1520

Prepared by Catherine King and Tim Benton for the Course Team

The Open University Press

Cover illustration: Piero della Francesca, *The Flagellation (Scala).*

The Open University Press
Walton Hall, Bletchley, Bucks.

First published 1972

Designed by the Media Development Group of the Open University

Printed in Great Britain by
EYRE AND SPOTTISWOODE LIMITED
AT GROSVENOR PRESS PORTSMOUTH

SBN 335 00653 1

This text forms part of the correspondence element of an Open University Second Level Course. The complete list of units in the course is given at the end of this text.

For general availability of supporting material referred to in this text, please write to the Director of Marketing, The Open University, Walton Hall, Bletchley, Bucks.

Further information on Open University courses may be obtained from the Admissions Office, The Open University, P.O. Box 48, Bletchley, Bucks.

INTRODUCTION

1   These three units (Units 8 and 10 by Catherine King and Unit 9 by Tim Benton) and the associated radio and television programmes, deal with the major characteristics of sculpture, architecture and painting in the early Renaissance, but each unit approaches the topic of a definition of the 'Renaissance' in rather a different way. The most general attempt to explore the definition of 'Renaissance' will be found in Unit 10 – on Painting. This unit asks whether the style of the period meant a return to classical principles or the creation of something 'new'. It uses paintings as examples but in many ways its arguments can stand for what was happening in sculpture and architecture as well. And the argument of the unit is in fact carried on in the next two units (11–12) – *Iconography* and *Artistic Status*.

2   The other two units in this block have a more precise scope. The theme of Unit 8 is the connection between techniques and materials, types of patronage and the prevailing ideology, and changing forms in sculpture. It is not a chronological treatment, nor does it give style-summaries or biographical information about individual artists. That treatment can be found in one of the set books: *The Art of the Renaissance* by P. and L. Murray. Unit 9, written by Tim Benton and Howard Burns, compares and contrasts the work of two of the most important fifteenth-century architects – Brunelleschi and Alberti, surveying the interaction between practice and theory in their work and the nature of, and extent to which, their ideal of antiquity created a new style of building.

3   Although we have chosen to treat sculpture, architecture and painting separately in this block, they are really very closely related in this period. Contemporaries grouped them under the heading *disegno* – the 'drawing' and 'design' which was felt their common factor. Artists themselves were usually 'jacks of all trades'. Ghiberti designed stained glass windows as well as the bronze doors of the Baptistry. The Pollaiuolo brothers painted and sculpted. Most architects, like Brunelleschi, were trained as sculptors – or more often, goldsmiths.

4   At this time there was little attempt to assign exclusive functions to sculpture, painting and architecture. Donatello produced sculptured reliefs which were nearly pictures. Ghirlandaio counterfeited bronze reliefs on the walls of the Sassetti Chapel, in paint. Sculptures were still often polychrome. This diversity of occupation was not at all new. Giotto had designed the Campanile and the fortifications of Florence in the fourteenth century. Arnolfo di Cambio had built and sculpted. The careers of Leonardo, Michelangelo and Raphael followed a similar pattern.

5   It was to emphasize this interdependence amongst the arts that we chose Piero della Francesca's *Flagellation* (probably painted between 1455 and 1461) for our front cover. The picture typifies the ideals of the time. The classical architecture in which the scene is set is the fulfilment of Alberti's dream. The perspective scheme is rigorously accurate and is enlivened by the eight realistically conceived 'personalities' who participate in the religious drama. The composition fulfils Alberti's *dictum* that a picture should be varied but not contain too many figures. Costume is half classical and half that of rich burgher classes in the fifteenth century. There are oddities in the classicism of the picture which are typical of the still somewhat confused ideals of the time: the seated

Roman official wears the hat of the Greek Emperor Paleologus who had recently visited Tuscany. His hat was the nearest Piero could get to recreating the Roman official's uniform. There is a little Tuscan tiled town house to the right. The column, topped by a bronze gilt figure, to which Christ is bound, represents that ideal of civic rhetorical sculpture which is much more than a decoration of a building and which Donatello tried to imitate. He had made a huge figure for a column of *Abundance* for the Old Market in Florence. It was carved in grey-stone or *pietra serena* and placed on a granite column taken from the Florentine Baptistry, which was thought at the time to be a classical temple. It has since disappeared. The sculpture in Piero's picture represents not only the fascination for bronze statuary, but the new but not often practised ideal that sculpture should be more independent of building and free-standing. So Piero's picture really represents the aspirations of architects, painters and sculptors: the interest in realism, perspective and the antique, and the way each art-form might contribute to creating a total 'classical' environment in harmony with religious ideals.

Radio and Television

6 RADIO PROGRAMME FOR UNIT 8. This programme is a talk given by Charles Avery, Assistant Keeper of the Victoria and Albert Musum Sculpture Department. He is also the author of one of the recommended books, *Florentine Renaissance Sculpture*. His talk will fill out my very brief survey of the character and significance of the patronage of sculpture in Part 1 of Unit 8.

TELEVISION AND RADIO PROGRAMMES FOR UNIT 9. Before you see and hear these programmes, please read Part 1 and Part 2 of Unit 9 up to paragraph 79, and familiarize yourself with the visual material (especially Figures 36–62) and with the accompanying notes (Appendix II) in this unit. Howard Burns, who lectures at the Courtauld Institute, has presented and written both the radio and television components for this unit. They are designed to survey Brunelleschi's Florentine architecture. The radio programme takes up the same theme as the television programme and inquires further into Brunelleschi's ideas, comparing the importance for his architecture of the antique, contained in the ruins he inspected in Rome, and the more recent architecture he knew in Tuscany and the Veneto.

RADIO PROGRAMME FOR UNIT 10. This programme is an illustrated talk by David Piper, the Director of the Fitzwilliam Museum at Cambridge. It is about the painter Piero della Francesca (1410/1420–1492) who, although not a Florentine artist but one who worked mainly in Umbria, absorbed the lessons of Alberti – even to the extent of writing a book on Perspective at the end of his life and thus matching the Albertian image of the artist-intellectual. You should have Plates 7–8 at hand, as well as the front cover of these units, when you listen to this programme.

There is also a television programme in Week 13 – 'The Development of *Fresco*' – which is highly relevant to Unit 10. It describes and reconstructs the technique of *fresco* painting and shows why this medium was so popular between about 1300 and 1500 in Tuscany, as well as why it declined after this period to such an extent that Vasari in the 1550s had to talk nostalgically of reviving it.

7 Throughout the block, paragraph, figure and plate numbers are consecutive, and we have used the same 'student stopper'. Try to identify it as you read Unit 9. Two appendices have been introduced: Appendix I, by Tim Benton, on Renaissance Perspective at the end of Unit 8 and Appendix II, which is a list of information about the illustrations in Unit 9, by Tim Benton and Howard Burns.

Set Books

8 The set books you will need for these units are: P. and L. Murray (1963) *The Art of the Renaissance*, Thames & Hudson, and E. Holt (1957) *A Documentary History of Art*, Volume I, Doubleday. The first will be referred to mainly for its illustrations in the form *Murray* and the relevant figure number. The second will be used for documentary references in the form *Holt* and the relevant page number. Any time you have to spare will be well spent reading the text of both these books.

R. Wittkower (1962) *Architectural Principles in the Age of Humanism*, Tiranti. (This will be referred to in the text as *Wittkower*.)

Recommended Reading

UNIT 8

9 Avery, Charles (1970) *Florentine Renaissance Sculpture*, J. Murray.
Seymour, Charles (1966) *Sculpture in Italy 1400–1500*, Penguin.

These two general surveys are well illustrated and well written. They both provide summaries of the styles and careers of major Florentine, and in the case of Seymour, Italian, sculptors.

Janson, Horst Woldemar (1957) *The sculpture of Donatello*, Princeton, Oxford University Press.
Krautheimer, Richard (1956) *Lorenzo Ghiberti*, Princeton, Oxford University Press.

Janson's book on Donatello is an up-to-date catalogue and a full photographic survey of his work. The catalogue items on Donatello's *Prophets*, his *David*, *Gattemelata*, *St. Peter receiving the Keys*, *The Feast of Herod*, the altar-piece at Padua, and *Judith and Holofernes* are especially interesting. Krautheimer's book on Ghiberti not only provides the latest and fullest survey of his work, but chapters are devoted to Ghiberti's contact with Alberti and his interest in the antique, which are very general in their import.

Ferguson, W. K. *et al.* (1962) *The Renaissance: Six Essays*, Harper and Row.

For this unit, the most important essay in this book is 'Hard Times and Investment in Culture' by R. S. Lopez.

UNIT 9

Anthony Blunt (1947) *Artistic Theory in Italy 1450–1600*, Oxford University Press; try to read the chapter on Alberti if you get the chance. Leon Battista Alberti, *Ten Books on Architecture*, ed. Joseph Rykwert, 1965, Tiranti; this modern reprint of the 1755 edition of Giacomo Leoni's translation into English of an Italian translation from Alberti's Latin, is unfortunately the only English translation available. Extracts from it are quoted in *Holt*. For a modern Italian translation, from which the extracts quoted in the unit are taken, see paragraph 94. *The Penguin Dictionary of Architecture*, 1967, Penguin, will be of assistance to you in the first part of the unit in learning the architectural terminology, but there are also useful articles on Renaissance architects. John Summerson (1964) *The Classical Language of Architecture*, Methuen, provides a broad but highly illuminating perspective to the way the classical tradition was passed on and adapted through European history. Vitruvius, *The Ten Books on Architecture*, trans. Morris Hicky Morgan, 1960, Dover, is a cheap and well illustrated and annotated edition, though the translation is not as reliable as the Frank Granger edition: Vitruvius, *On Architecture*, 2 vols., ed. Frank Granger, 1962, Harvard University Press. Peter Murray (1971) *The Architecture of the Italian Renaissance*, Thames and Hudson, provides a general survey of Renaissance architecture, with some useful illustrations. If you get a chance to read the first three chapters, you would be able to broaden the specific treatment given here. Another good general work is, Bates Lowry (1968) *Renaissance Architecture*, Studio Vista. Finally, one of the few books devoted entirely to Alberti in the English language: Joan Gadol (1969) *Leon Battista Alberti, Universal Man of the Early Renaissance*, University of Chicago Press, covers a very wide range of Alberti's theoretical writing and fills in the background to Renaissance thought and the arts. It is a valuable summary of the huge Alberti literature.

For Brunelleschi, the best source is Antonio di Tuccio Manetti (1970) *The Life of Brunelleschi*, with introduction, notes and critical text by Howard Saalman. His introduction and notes contain a great deal of additional information. The English translation is unfortunately not altogether accurate. Further valuable information can be found in Frank D. Prager and Gustina Scaglia (1970) *Brunelleschi: Studies of his Technology and Inventions*, M.I.T. Press.

For Brunelleschi's perspective discoveries, see John White (1967) *The Birth and Rebirth of Pictorial Space*, Faber. For Brunelleschi's architectural sources, Howard Burns, 'Quattrocento architecture and the antique: some problems', in R. R. Bolgar (1971) (ed.), *Classical Influence in European Culture, A.D. 500–1500*, Cambridge University Press.

The long-awaited volume in the Pelican History of Art series should be published in 1972 or early 1973: L. H. Heydenreich and W. Lotz, *Architecture in Italy, 1400–1600*. This will contain a full discussion of both Brunelleschi's and Alberti's architecture.

UNIT 10

Antal, Frederick (1947) *Florentine painting and its social background*, Routledge and Kegan Paul.
Meiss, Meillard (1964) *Painting in Florence and Siena after the Black Death: the arts, religion and society in the middle fourteenth century*, Harper and Row.

Both these books survey the connection between a change in style of painting and in style of life. The book by Meiss has the narrower scope and can be read less critically than the Antal. However, the Antal, despite its sometimes oversimplified 'Marxist' approach, is an important and stimulating book.

Alberti, Leon Battista, *On painting*, trans. John R. Spencer, 1966, Yale University Press.

Alberti's *Treatise on Painting* is the most important verbal document we possess for the art theory of the fifteenth century in Florence. You should bear in mind however, that much of his 'advice' to painters was not heeded until the sixteenth and seventeenth centuries.

White, John (1967) *The Birth and Rebirth of Pictorial Space*, Faber.

John White describes the development of perspective in the fourteenth and fifteenth centuries in Tuscany. This is not just a description of the adoption of Brunelleschian perspective. It also explains the formal, emotional and compositional pitfalls and advantages of 'the new perspective', and emphasizes how partial a 'realism' it created in paintings.

Borsook, E. (1960) *The Mural Painters of Tuscany*, Phaidon.
Meiss, Meillard (1970) *The Great Age of Fresco*, Phaidon.

These two books are about *fresco* painting. The one by Borsook is the only book which provides photographs of *fresco* in its architectural setting, as well as an introduction to and catalogue to the major frescoes illustrated. The book by Meiss is chiefly valuable for its photographs which are more lavish than those in Borsook, and because it covers classical *fresco* paintings as well.

Clark, Kenneth (1969) *Piero della Francesca: Complete Edition of the paintings*, Phaidon.
Pope-Hennessy, John (1969) *Paolo Uccello*, Phaidon.

These are two monographs devoted to individual artists. Like Krautheimer's and Janson's books on sculpture they provide valuable general information.

Berenson, Bernhard (1969) *The Italian painters of the Renaissance*, Collins: Fontana.

Berenson's book is hardly a reflection of the most up to date conclusions on Florentine painting. However, it is a 'classic' of its kind.

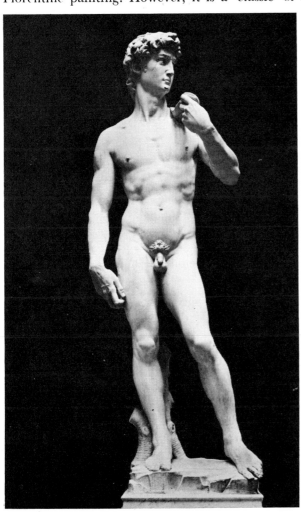

Figure 1

UNIT 8   FLORENTINE SCULPTURAL TECHNIQUES AND STYLISTIC CHANGES

10   In this unit I shall describe some of the main developments in sculpture between 1402 and 1470 or so and offer some explanation for their occurrence, I shall then describe the techniques of carving and casting in some detail. concentrating on marble and bronze sculpture, and explaining how technical problems influenced criticism, the value placed on work and the role of the artist and patron. Finally I shall examine some examples of 'developments' in the sculpture of this time more specifically. This final section will therefore 'fill out' the outline presented in the first, introductory section.

List of Contents

Part 1   A short survey and explanation of some of the significant changes which took place in Florentine sculpture between 1402 and 1470: Decorating buildings; Money and Sculpture; From the dark tomb to light; Technical innovations; Presumption and Prestige, and Competitions and Competitiveness.

Part 2   Techniques and Materials: their importance for patronage and working conditions

Part 3   Developments in Florentine Sculpture:
   (i)   Sculpture, ideology and church furniture
   (ii) New types of statuary and relief

Appendix I   Renaissance Perspective

Figures for Unit 8

12   1   *David*, Michelangelo, marble, 1503, Accademia, Florence. (*Mansell Collection*)

2   *St. Peter receiving the Keys of Heaven*, Donatello, marble, 1425–30. (*Victoria and Albert Museum*)

3   A bow-drill.

4   Bronze casting techniques.

5   *Virgin with a Laughing Child*, Antonio Rossellino, *terracotta*, before 1479. (*Victoria and Albert Museum*)

6   *Perseus and Medusa*, Benvenuto Cellini, trial model in bronze, 1554. (*Victoria and Albert Museum*)

7   A *terracotta* roundel, school of Luca della Robbia. (*Mansell Collection*)

8   'T' Square and wooden cage for transferring measurements.

9   Alberti's method of transferring measurements.

10   Sculptor's tools.

11   The effect of the *scarpello* and *calcagnuolo*: *The Rondanini Pietà*, Michelangelo. (*Mansell Collection*)

12   *St. Michael*, a follower of Pisano, marble. (*Victoria and Albert Museum*)

13   *Abraham and Isaac*, Donatello, marble, 1421, Museo del Opera, Florence. (*Mansell Collection*)

14   *Judith and Holofernes*, Donatello, bronze, 1457–1460, Piazza della Signoria, Florence. (*Mansell Collection*)

15   *St. John the Evangelist*, Donatello, marble, 1408–15, Museo del Opera, Florence. (*Mansell Collection*)

16   *St. Luke*, Nanni di Banco, marble, 1408–15, Museo del Opera, Florence. (*Mansell Collection*)

17   *Tomb for Pope John XXIII*, Donatello, 1424–27, Baptistry, Florence. (*Mansell Collection*)

18   *The Orso Monument*, marble, 1323 (a reconstruction).

19   *The Third Bronze Doors*, Ghiberti, 1430–1452, Baptistry, Florence. (*Mansell Collection*)

20   *A bust of Chellini*, Antonio Rossellino, marble, 1456. (*Victoria and Albert Museum*)

21   *Hercules and Antaeus*, Pollaiuolo, bronze, 1475?, Bargello, Florence. (*Mansell Collection*)

22   *Habbakuk*, Donatello, marble, 1427–35, Museo del Opera, Florence. (*B.B.C.*)

23   *The Feast of Herod*, Donatello, bronze, 1423–27, Font, Siena Cathedral. (*Mansell Collection*)

24   *A Prisoner*, Michelangelo, marble, Galleria Antica e Moderna, Florence. (*Mansell Collection*)

PART I   A SURVEY AND EXPLANATION OF SOME OF THE SIGNIFICANT CHANGES WHICH TOOK PLACE IN FLORENTINE SCULPTURE BETWEEN 1402 AND 1470

13   During the period roughly limited by the date 1402 (when Ghiberti began the second bronze doors for the Florentine Baptistry) and the date 1466 or so (when Donatello died), Florentine sculptors took over the lead in Italian sculpture from the Pisans and Venetians. Workmen from these two cities had cast the first bronze doors for the Baptistry in the mid-fourteenth century. Between 1402 and 1453, Ghiberti and his numerous assistants made the second and third pairs of doors in conscious rivalry with the first pair. When the final pair were ready they were given pride of place, opposite the central door of the new cathedral. Their success was a symbol of the fact that Florentine sculptors had 'arrived' and could now hold their own against all-comers. I want to explain how this success story was possible in terms of the building activity of the fourteenth century, new types of patronage, fascination with classical culture, technical innovations and (most inexplicable of all) a new self-consciousness and competitiveness amongst sculptors.

14   During this period Florentine sculptors revolutionized the treatment of relief and statuary. They cast the first large bronze niche figures and the first free-standing statutes since antiquity. They adopted the new perspective of Brunelleschi and Alberti and borrowed from classical sculpture for their proportions and figures. Donatello and Ghiberti initiated the habit of a journey to Rome which became compulsory for so many artists until the nineteenth century. Artists experimented with life-casts and death masks and produced extremely realistic portraiture. They created new types of relief sculpture.

Especially important was Donatello's *rilievo stiacciato* or 'flattened relief' which attempts to rival painting in its creation of space and depth on a virtually flat surface.

15   It was a period too which saw an increase in contact between scholars and artists, especially sculptors like Ghiberti and Donatello, becoming interested in antiquity under the guidance of their humanist friends. It was this 'intellectual' atmosphere which is probably behind Ghiberti's *Commentaries* written in the 1440s, which is really the first attempt by an artist to write the History of Art, and an autobiography. An immense amount of sculpture, and a great variety was produced. Most important commissions focussed on the decoration of the new Cathedral and the Baptistry opposite it (which was dedicated to the patron saint of Florence, St. John the Baptist), the Medici parish Church of San Lorenzo, and the niche statuary for the Guild Church of Or San Michele.

Decorating buildings

16   The fourteenth century had been a major period of building in Florence, as John Larner has described (Unit 7). During the fifteenth century many of the sculptural 'finishing touches' were added, in the external and internal decoration of these buildings with pulpits, doors, tombs, niche statuary and decorative reliefs. So, in a sense, the sculptural activity in this period was a natural consequence of the great building plans of the previous century and of the ebullient rivalry with other cities which had been behind the building of the Cathedral and the beginnings of town planning in Florence. But it was not just the result of a 'spin-off' of building activity.

Money and sculpture

17   Marble and bronze sculpture cost a lot and they were more durable than other materials. The merchant patrons of fifteenth-century Florence liked costly monuments, because that meant prestige, *and* they could afford them. They wanted to display their wealth, and the value of their 'gift' to the community, and they wanted memorials to their power, and aristocratic 'cultured' taste, which would last. Durability was certainly a major concern, as one can tell in this letter from Niccolo Acciaiuoli to his brother, in 1356:

> Whatever else God has granted me will go to my descendants and I know not whom: this Monastery and its decorations alone belong to me for all time to come, and will preserve my name in my country. And if the soul is immortal, as Monsignor the Chancellor says, then my soul, wherever it is ordered to go, will delight in this building.
> From Antal, F. (1947) *Florentine Painting and its Social Background*, Routledge and Kegan Paul, p. 132.

18   Bronze was more durable than marble, as well as costing about ten times as much as an equivalent statue in marble. It was so expensive that the contract for Ghiberti's bronze *St. Matthew* in 1419 for the Banker's Guild niche in Or San Michele, specifies the weight of the statue to the nearest pound (*Murray*, Figure 22). But marble was expensive too, for it had to be transported from the Apuan Mountains to Florence. Even sculptors as well known as Michelangelo or Donatello had to 'make do' with flawed blocks, because they were available in Florence. Michelangelo's huge marble *David* was carved out of a block which had already been worked and cracked (Figure 1). That is perhaps the

explanation for the rather cramped position of the backmost leg. Donatello's relief of *St. Peter receiving the Keys of Heaven* has little 'knots' and a diagonal grey streak on its surface, which the sculptor obviously wouldn't have chosen ideally (Figure 2). The sheer prestige of being able to afford bronze or marble really did matter to patrons. There is a good example of this in the inscription on a tabernacle commissioned by the Medici family in the church of *SS. Annunziata* which reads, 'The marble alone cost four thousand florins'. Bronze and marble sculpture tempted 'up and coming' merchants, and its development during this period must be linked with Florentine capitalism. Typically, the huge amounts of bronze needed for the bronze doors for the Baptistry came from Flanders, the commercial partner of Florence in the field of the wool trade and banking business.

19 Still, the relationship between money and sculpture is really more subtle than this. It was not just a question of spending surplus profits, but expiating the guilt of usury (the accumulation of profit by lending money at interest) in spending 'ill-gotten gains' for the benefit of the Church and the community at large. R. S. Lopez in an essay on 'Hard times and investment in culture' in *The Renaissance: Six Essays* (see paragraph 9) has argued that the 'nouveaux riches' of fifteenth-century Florence invested in culture, as merchants in other countries invested in land, to become 'aristocratic'. The nature and motives of sculptural patronage will be dealt with in detail by Charles Avery in the radio programme for this week.

From the dark tomb to light

20 One very important factor determining the development of sculpture in this period, was contemporary fascination with the culture of classical Rome. One reason why artists and patrons liked Carrara marble was because it was the nearest equivalent to the Parian marble so highly prized in classical times. They liked bronze because the classical writers Pliny and Vitruvius had praised it. Interest in classical art was by no means new, as I explain at greater length in Unit 10, Part 1, but it was more thoroughgoing than previously. Artists and humanists like Lorenzetti and Petrarch in the fourteenth century had enthused over classical remains. Petrarch had wandered on the Capitol in Rome with his politician friend Cola di Rienzo, dreaming of a new Italy, unified under a Republic. But by the fifteenth century these political hopes were dashed, and it has been suggested that this disappointment channelled ambition more narrowly towards recreating Roman civilization in the 'safer' spheres of art and literature. Archaeological interest really began in the fifteenth century. Artists like Brunelleschi and Donatello, artist-intellectuals like Alberti, humanist administrators like Bracciolini and Bruni and businessmen like Niccolò Niccoli, Vespasiano da Bisticci and Cyriac of Ancona all became fascinated by classical remains. It is particularly interesting that such businessmen were coming to interest themselves in antiquity. There had been some enthusiasm for classical objects before the fifteenth century, but invariably from scholarly clerics. But in the early part of the century there was something of a split between the humanists who were really interested in the philology of Roman inscriptions (that is how the grammar and style of inscriptions could help them purify their Latin), and artists looking for new motifs and techniques. Alberti, was, as usual, peculiar in straddling the two camps. This interest meant that more and more objects, buildings (and very late in the Renaissance, paintings) were made available to artists.

21   The early fifteenth-century fascination with classical civilization and art was profoundly emotional: bound up with the feeling that if scholars and artists could reconstruct the glory of this past civilization of Italy, they could re-live the cultural and political triumphs of that past. Archaeology was at this time in fact very much like a relic hunt, with the same indiscriminating zeal and belief in the 'power' objects had, in themselves. Cyriac of Ancona, a Florentine businessman who travelled all over Asia Minor in the 1420s collecting drawings and inscriptions vowed that he would 'wake the dead'; that he would 'revive the glorious things which were alive to the living in antiquity but had become buried and defunct through the lapse of ages and persistent injury at the hands of the half-dead; to bring them from the dark tomb to light, to live once more among living men'. (C. Mitchell (1960) 'Archaeology and Romance', in *Italian Renaissance Studies*, Faber, p. 470.)

22   Now read an extract from Ghiberti's *Commentaries* (*Holt*, pp. 158–66) and decide what aspects of classical art interested this sculptor.

Well, Ghiberti appreciates the realism of the carved figures, the Roman lettering, the general technical skill *and* the subject matter – the symbolism – of what he had seen. He is interested in form, content, techniques *and* the idealized grace of treatment. Just how much he or any other artist at the time was able to reproduce these features will be examined later, in Unit 10.

Technical innovations

23   One specific classical revival – the use of the classical bow-drill in marble sculpture was all-important. The bow-drill (Figure 3) had been used sporadically throughout the Middle Ages and increasingly after the thirteenth century, but it became indispensable in the fifteenth century, and really effective when hard tempered steel was made available by the metallurgical revolution of the thirteenth century. The bow-drill allows the sculptor to cut out large amounts of marble very quickly and make holes through the block without cracking it. Most medieval sculptors used abrasion (rubbing and chipping) to make the desired shape and because this produces a rough surface, polychrome was often used. It was the bow-drill which enabled a sculptor to reproduce the classical effects of deep undercutting in drapery or facial features, freer forms (the arm wide of the body, legs apart) and delicate, precise detail. Treatment of curling hair was especially important. These techniques will be explained in Part 2.

24   The sheer fact that Ghiberti cast the two bronze doors during this period was important too. This enterprise was large enough to warrant a foundry of its own and almost every important sculptor including Donatello passed through his workshop at one time or another. The workshop was something of a school for bronze casters. Whereas the first bronze doors made by Ghiberti had been cast in many little pieces like the early pair by Pisano, and figures and scenes had been bolted onto a flat background, the final pair of doors had eight panels, each cast as a whole.

Now pause and compare a panel from the first doors by Ghiberti, and from his second doors (*Murray*, Figures 17, 23). What has Ghiberti's technical innovation enabled him to do?

Figure 2

In the second panel of *The Story of Joseph* he has been able to treat the whole
panel, filling it with many incidents and many more gradations of depth. There
is no abrupt transition between foreground and background as there must be
when a scene is pinned onto a flat background. Ghiberti's workshop then,
experimented and perfected casting methods, and this allowed for greater
subtlety of effect, and the use of Alberti's perspective constructions (Appendix I).

Presumption and prestige

25 Rather specialized conditions encouraged the development of bronze sculpture.
In 1416 the City Council of Florence decreed that the guilds should be
allowed to commission bronze rather than marble statues for the niches of Or
San Michele. Previously law and custom reserved bronze for specific religious
patronage. Even in the 1450s when Donatello made a large equestrian statue
of a *condottiere*, a secular military hero, in Padua, it was probably thought rather
presumptuous (*Murray*, Figure 32). The use of bronze, and of marble, was still
something of a privilege connected with the Sumptuary Laws which laid down
what sort of clothes or houses were suitable to different classes in society.
Equestrian statues in bronze had been customarily reserved for the monuments
of Emperors like that of Marcus Aurelius, but Donatello made one for a
condottiere. Similarly we find someone grumbling in a dialogue on art written
by Petrarch in the 1350s that memorials were once 'erected in the honour of
wise and learned men . . . and nowadays they are erected unto ryche Mer-
chantes, wrought of outlandish marble, of great value' (M. Baxandall (1971)
Giotto and the Orators, Oxford University Press, p. 57). Filarete, who wrote a
treatise on art in the fifteenth century, speaks of marble being best used for
statues of saints, celebrated men and tombs.

Competitions and competitiveness

26 Of course, this is a very generalized explanation of how sculpture in bronze and
stone developed during this period. Basically the most important factors seem
to have been the availability of surplus capital and interest in antiquity at this
time. One other very important feature of sculpture at this time must be
mentioned. This is the very strong element of virtuoso display, competitiveness
and the consciousness amongst sculptors that they were playing a role in the
exploration and improvement of their art. These features have been jointly
termed 'the idea of progress' by E. H. Gombrich, and they have a lot to do

with the feeling that a 'renaissance' or 'rebirth' was happening, though it is very difficult to tell whether they are a cause or an effect of developments in sculpture at this time.

Now read the art-theorist Alberti's description of the state of Florentine art in 1435 (*Holt*, pp. 205–6). Does it display self-consciousness of a revival? Read as well Ghiberti's description of how he won the competition for the Baptistry doors in 1402 (*Holt*, pp. 156–63). How do competitions affect the sculptor?

The habit of setting competitions for a commission, which really started in Florence in 1402, is partly a convenient way of choosing an artist, but it is also an ostentatious display that nothing but the best is good enough for the patrons. It created a situation where artists, whenever they worked side by side (as Donatello and della Robbia did in the sculpting of the *Cantorie* (*Murray*, Figures 29, 175)) tended to try and do better – to be 'different'.

27   The element of virtuoso display was connected with such competitiveness. It is typified by Donatello's insertion of little perspective exercises in the partition wall behind the main scene of *The Feast of Herod* (Figure 23). Can you see the carefully contrived 'flues' in the pattern of the brickwork? They have nothing to do with the 'story'. Another example is Ghiberti's technical display in casting each of the eight panels for his second Baptistry doors as a whole. Possibly too, he adopted elongated proportions for the figures in these panels in conscious display that he was as good as the ancient Greek sculptor Lysippus whom he had read about in Pliny's *Natural History*. These sorts of display were part 'problem-solving' for art's sake and part self-advertising, possibly with an eye for the next commission. This probably increased interest in 'being different' and therefore influenced the developments of this period.

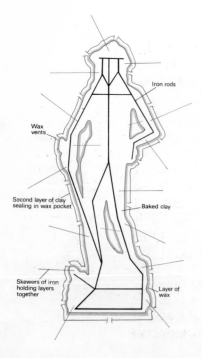

Iron rods

Wax vents

Second layer of clay sealing in wax pocket

Baked clay

Skewers of iron holding layers together

Layer of wax

Figure 4

PART II   TECHNIQUES AND MATERIALS: THEIR IMPORTANCE FOR PATRONAGE AND WORKING CONDITIONS

28   It is only too easy to talk about Florentine sculpture as though *terracotta* (literally 'terracocta' – cooked or baked earth) and marble, bronze, sandstone and wood were all the same thing. 'Sculpture' is a misleading term too, for bronze is moulded and it is only really stone and wood which are cut out.

EXERCISE

29   To begin with, though, I want you to find out what you know or can guess about how sculpture was done. Here are some questions to help your self-analysis. Considering these materials: wood, bronze, marble, sandstone and *terracotta*, wax, clay:

1   Which was the most expensive in the fifteenth century?
2   If you were a rich merchant which material would you choose to commission?
3   If you have to sculpt a rearing horse or a figure balanced on one leg with his arms flung out, which material would you prefer to work with?
4   If you weren't quite sure about the shape you wanted in your figure or panel, which material would you choose to work with?
5   If you wanted to sculpt a figure to stand outside in all weathers, which material would you choose and what could you do to any of the materials to make them more durable?

I shall answer these questions in paragraph 42.

Casting: Bronze (summarized in Figure 4)

30   Casting was the main method of making bronze statues and panels at this period. There are detailed descriptions of the process in Vasari's preface to *The Lives of the Artists* and in Cellini's *Art of Goldsmithing and Sculpture*. These were both written in the sixteenth century. There is some treatment in Cennini's fourteenth-century *Handbook for the Craftsman*. The process is called *cire perdu* or 'lost wax' because bronze is poured into a space created by melting out wax, and it is *not* special to the Renaissance. To begin with, the sculptor makes little sketch models in wax and soft clay. They often show the sort of freedom of touch and suggestive vagueness that a modern spectator finds attractive. When he had decided on one model the sculptor would usually finish it in clay and bake it. Antonio Rossellino's *Virgin with a laughing Child* (Figure 5) is probably one of these models. Few of them survive. Sometimes they would be in bronze like the little trial-models Cellini made in 1554 for his huge *Perseus and Medusa* (Figure 6). At this stage the patron would probably be asked to approve further investment.

31   To create the mould the little model had to be enlarged to nearly the desired size for the final statue or panel. It would be in clay strengthened with iron

Figure 5

Figure 11

Figure 7

Figure 6

rods and would be baked several times to ensure complete dryness. In the sixteenth century it was the practice to take a plaster mould off the baked clay statue in numbered sections so that the sculptor could create replicas in cheaper material, and so that he could remake his statue if the bronze mould went wrong. This may have been so in the fifteenth century. The next stage was to cover the clay statue (now *terracotta* as it had been baked) with a uniform layer (about a finger's width) of wax, taking care to reproduce on the surface of the wax all the detail required on the surface of the bronze. This wax skin was then covered in plaster so as to create a strong envelope. The whole was pinned together with metal rods so that the various layers would not slip out of alignment. Vents would have been made for the wax pocket to the exterior and between various parts of the statue or panel so that the wax could flow out, bronze could flow in and enter every crevice of the mould, and any air could be expressed. The final firing was often done by bell-founders. The composition of bronze was roughly two parts of copper to one part brass, but there was a lot of variation. Cellini described with great relish throwing all the pewter plates in his dinner service into the furnace when his molten bronze curdled. His *Perseus* was a very successful cast.

32   The completed cast would often be imperfect and have lumps of bronze sticking out where the vents had been. These had to be sawn off and polished down. Holes had to be left to extract the clay core and then filled in. Details of hair, of facial expression or drapery would probably need redefinition with chisels and punches. Acid might be used to turn the bronze green or it might be varnished to preserve its blackness. Or it might be painted. All these finishes (except the application of acid) increased the durability of the sculpture.

33   Both Vasari and Cellini speak as though figures were cast as a whole. We know this was not the case in the fifteenth century. Donatello's *St. John the Baptist* was cast in three pieces, his *Judith and Holofernes* in eleven, and his *St. Louis of Toulouse* in many sections which were bolted together. The process involved in creating a *terracotta* sculpture has already been partly described. It was essentially baked clay painted with glazes of various colours. Quite often it was regarded as a cheap substitute for marble and painted white, but the *terracotta* of Luca Della Robbia was many-coloured and used for elaborate monuments (Figure 7).

Marble and wood carving (see Figures 8-11)

34   The most highly-prized stone for sculpture was the marble which came from the mountains north of Pisa, especially the white marble of Carrara which was of fine texture and came in wide strata. *Pietra serena* (a grey-blue sandstone) was also extensively used for sculptural decoration. It came from the hills near to Florence – from Settignano, Maiano, and Fiesole.

35   Stone sculptors began work just as bronze casters did, with small clay or wax models. We know from Cellini that Donatello at least, began work on the block at this point, tracing out the views of the little figure on the four sides of the the block (or on the one face if it was a relief) and chipping or drilling out each 'outline' until he had the rough shape of a figure. Tremendous precision was required with this method, in transferring the design of the small model to a large block. Some sculptors used a simple 'T' square or placed a wooden box 'cage' over the big block and the little model standing side by side (Figure 8). Proportions could then be transferred quite easily. Incidentally this technical procedure helps to explain the fascination of sculptors at this time with the simple canons of classical sculpture, which will be described in Unit 10. Other

sculptors may have used a very accurate method, designed by the Florentine art-theorist Alberti for measuring antique statues, and developed from surveyors' instruments (Figure 9).

Cellini, in the sixteenth century, spoke disapprovingly of these methods. He preferred the more cautious method of creating a model to the required size which could be placed next to the block. He tells us that Michelangelo used both methods and finally preferred the latter. Perhaps early fifteenth-century sculptors used both methods too. Still, in *fresco* painting (about which there is a television programme in Week 13), during the fifteenth century the trend was towards greater and greater precision and more and more preparatory work, at the end of the century, whereas the earlier painters had worked straight on the wall. So the idea of Donatello and his contemporaries cutting straight into the stone with only a little clay sketch as a guide is more probable.

EXERCISE

Look now at Figure 10, which illustrates sculptor's tools at this time. For what purpose would each tool be used? Which would be associated with what effects?

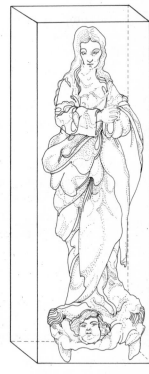

Figure 8

36   The block was roughed out using a *subbia* (a) (Figure 10) at an oblique angle to the block to prevent 'bruising' (that is star-shaped cracks) or a bow-drill (b) which was the quickest way to get rid of, say, the huge mass of stone between a raised arm and a torso. When the statue's final surface was about a finger's breadth away 'inside' the block, the *scarpello*, *gradina* and *calcagnuolo* were used (d, c). These are toothed and produced the rough surface sometimes seen on the backs of figures or on the unfinished work of Michelangelo (Figure 11). Cellini and Vasari describe this stage very enthusiastically. Cellini describes it as like drawing on the surface of the shape rather as if it was like 'shading in' an outline. When this had been completed files (e) would be used for further smoothing and then the final detail and under-cutting – the thin sweep of drapery or a deep fold, the holes for pupils, ears, curling hair or beard, nose,

mouth or hands – were often done with a smaller bow-drill. With this deep grooves could be created by making a series of holes and then breaking down the little bridges between them. It is very easy to see the marks of the drill in Figure 12.

37   Finally, the sculpture would be polished with bunches of straw and pumice stone. Polish protected the marble. It prevented water from settling, and rotting into the grain of the stone. It brought out colour and the veining in the stone and it allowed the sculptor to highlight the shapes, putting extra polish where a painter would put light or white paint. For instance, he would polish a cheek highly, but leave the eye socket a little duller in texture, to give it extra depth. Or 'flesh' would be highly polished, whereas drapery or hair would be left a little rougher.

38   Wood sculpture followed a similar pattern to that of marble carving. Like sandstone, it was much easier to work than marble, but was less durable. Donatello's *St. Mary Magdalen* (*Murray*, Figure 2) shows the fine detail and complicated outline available to the wood carver. But wood sculptures had to be made out of many pieces of relatively soft wood at this time. The import of large pieces of carvable wood from Africa and America came much later. Wood sculpture was also very often painted, like *terracotta*, with what we would probably feel garish results. Donatello's statue was painted by him at one time.

Figure 9

EXERCISE

A comparison between marble and bronze sculpture

39   I want you to compare the effects of bronze and marble in terms of Donatello's *Abraham and Isaac* (Figure 13) made to stand in a niche high on the wall of the Cathedral and his *Judith and Holofernes* (Figure 14) probably made as the central figure for a free-standing fountain. These sculptures both represent a scene of intended killing: Abraham about to sacrifice his son Isaac and Judith about to kill her seducer, the tyrant King Holofernes. You should take the fact that the two sculptures were intended for different functions into account in your comparison. Try to decide which material (marble or bronze) has been used for each and note down any points about, for example, pose, complexity of detail, overall shape, function, that would support your decision.

DISCUSSION

40   Fundamentally the detail of the Judith is much the more delicate and complex. The poses of the figures too display more variety. The outline is much more variable. But, of course, the *Abraham* was made to stand in a narrow niche at a great height. It had to fit a pre-determined shape and make an impact at a distance. Weathering may account for the loss of precision in details, although of course that only shows that marble is more susceptible to erosion than bronze. Still, there are certain things Donatello couldn't have reproduced in stone, even if he had made a marble fountain figure. He couldn't have carved the outstretched arm and thin sword blade of *Judith* in stone. He

19

would have had to get round the problem in keeping the arm close to the body and laying the knife blade against the neck of the 'victim', as he did in his *Abraham*, so that he could just draw the outline of the knife against the solid block of stone. Did you notice too that Isaac's chin is pulled in, and his whole body twisted round to fit the central core of stone? One is conscious all the time that the stone figures had to stand inside the predetermined shape of the block, as well as the niche. Isaac's leg too could never jut free and hang in space as one of Holofernes' does. Imagine how difficult it would be to carve out an unsupported shape like this without snapping it off – let alone the problem of moving it. In the *Judith* it was easy to define the ruckles and pleats of drapery, the ridges of veins or hair and the points where 'bone' is close to 'skin'. Detail had been moulded out of soft wax and molten, flowing bronze had taken these shapes easily. Nor does bronze break; at the worst it dents and bends. Michelangelo said (so Vasari tells us) that a really 'good' statue should be capable of being rolled down a hillside without breaking. He was making a virtue of the necessity of marble sculpture. But it is true that the flowing simple outline of the *Abraham* – the compactness and tightness of every shape in relation to a central core – gives it tremendous conviction and unity.

41   Ultimately, the marble worker is much more limited than the bronze caster. He has to hew out shape, translating his little wax or soft clay models into hard stone. He works from outside inwards to an imagined shape somewhere inside the block. He has to follow the grain of his stone, avoid flaws or cracks and work within predetermined dimensions. The bronze caster builds up shapes from a central core. He begins with an iron skeleton of rods and covers that with clay flesh. These are, in fact, the terms Vasari uses – like anatomical dissection in reverse. It is very probable that bronze sculptors thought in terms of 'clothing' a skeleton, in their large clay model. On the head-dress just above the forehead of Judith there are marks of cloth. It looks as though Donatello actually draped his clay model with *real cloth* and because he didn't give it a sufficiently thick coat of clay on top, the wax and then the bronze 'took' the texture. That means that bronze sculptors could cheat in counterfeiting nature. They could take life-casts and death-masks and use them to mould bronze. Perhaps this comparison shows why bronze sculpture was so sought after, and praised during the fifteenth century. Now check back on, and if necessary revise, your answers to the exercise in paragraph 29.

42   **SPECIMEN ANSWERS TO THE QUESTIONS IN PARAGRAPH 29**

   1   In this order; bronze, marble, sandstone and wood, *terracotta*.

   2   Bronze, with marble as second best.

   3   Bronze, or possibly wood if you were prepared to do a lot of joining.

   4   Wax or clay: no fifteenth-century sculptor worth his salt or his patronage began work on expensive materials until he knew what he wanted to do.

   5   Bronze or marble, but with careful polishing or painting, wood or *terracotta* would be quite durable.

   EXERCISE

43   This exercise is something of a rag-bag. I want you to come to some conclusions about the way techniques and materials affected the value of work, the type of patronage required, the 'authorship' of autograph work and the position and status of the sculptor. I have chosen some 'evidence' to assist you in answering these questions. Read through the information and the questions below and make your decisions before reading on. This should take you about fifteen minutes.

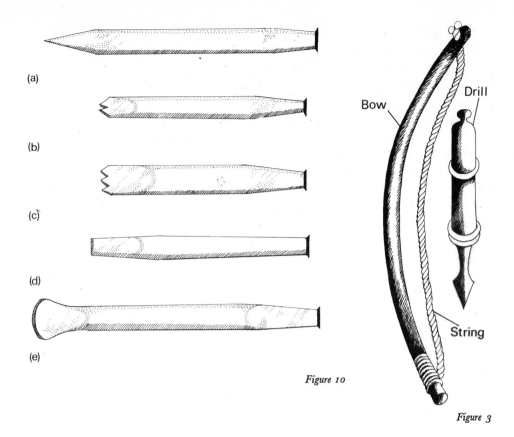

(a)

(b)

(c)

(d)

(e)

Figure 10

Bow

Drill

String

Figure 3

Information and questions

1   What was the status of the sculptor at this time – was he an artisan, or a gentleman?

(a)   Three of the most famous sculptors in the late fifteenth century were called Mino da Fiesole, Desiderio da Settignano and Benedetto da Maiano (that is, Benedetto from the village of Maiano, etc. . .).

(b)   Stone blocks were often roughed out in the quarries before being transported to Florence.

Clue word: *pietra serena*

2   Artists like Donatello inscribed their names on their sculptures. What sort of claims were they thereby making about their contribution to the sculpture?

(a)   The twin bronze pulpits for San Lorenzo were commissioned by the Medici from Donatello in the 1460s. They were finished in 1470 or so. Donatello died in 1466 (*Murray*, Figure 36).

(b)   In 1402 Ghiberti won the competition for the commission to make the second bronze Baptistry doors. He began work at once and signed a contract in 1407 when he became a Master. The head of his workshop signed the contract in 1403.

(c)   Pomponio Guarico wrote in 1504 that Donatello knew little about the art of bronze casting. He had his statues cast by bronze founders.

3   What was the artist paid for?
Compare these statues: one by Donatello, of *St. John the Evangelist*, and the other by Nanni di Banco of *St. Luke*. (Figures 15, 16.)
They were both carved in marble, to stand side by side in two niches, between 1408 and 1415. Donatello got more money. Why?

4   Finally, on the evidence of information I have given you in Parts 1 and 2, would you expect individual patrons to have commissioned much sculpture?

21

DISCUSSION

44   1   You probably guessed that these sculptors came from stone-cutters' families living in the main quarry areas near Florence. This fact emphasizes how very close still was the link between stone-cutting and sculpting and how very 'artisan-like' were the sculptor's labours.

45   2   Although the fifteenth century in Florence seems to be the great period for individual innovation and was certainly a time when individual sculptors had great public prestige (Ghiberti's bronze doors were extremely *political* in their importance), most work was undertaken collaboratively. Although Ghiberti had won his commission it was quite acceptable that as he was not yet a 'master' of a workshop, he did not sign 'his' contract. It is typical too that 'Donatello's' pulpits could be finished after his death by his assistants. Bronze and stone sculpture involved such labour that collaborative work was essential. We are not, after all, used to sculptures which take fifty years to complete. This is how long Ghiberti and his assistants worked on the two pairs of Bronze doors for the Baptistry. Only collaborative work could ensure the production of such huge sculptures and the 'handing down' of complicated techniques. Many sculptural projects were in fact like building programmes in their vastness, and sculptors could, as Donatello did, feel that the responsibility for drawing up specifications (even though the work might be handed over to others at various stages as an architect hands over the details to builders) was enough to warrant the claim that a sculpture was 'his'. Twentieth-century artists like Moholy Nagy who insisted that work was his because *he* had given his specifications to a factory are, in fact, part of a longer tradition than those critics who believe that the autograph work must be totally the result of one man's work.

46   3   Most payments took into account the amount of work put into a sculpture. Donatello got more money than Nanni di Banco because he had undercut his statue more. You can see this especially in the drapery over the knees of *St. John the Evangelist* (Figure 15). Undercutting, as you remember, meant cutting deep into a block and involved courage and concentration. The appreciation of the value of technical skill underlies most Renaissance criticism of sculpture. Perhaps because this period was one of such expansion in techniques and variety of shapes tackled, there was tremendous admiration for overcoming difficulties: for creating something out of nothing. Hence the interest in Michelangelo's ability to carve his *David* out of a cracked block of marble, or in Ghiberti's innovations in relief casting.

47   4   Work on sculpture was undertaken collaboratively, and so was patronage. Because sculpture took so long and cost so much, responsibility for patronage had to be corporate. Individual patronage is quite unusual at this period, and then it concentrated on cheaper materials like *terracotta*, or small objects like little bronze ornaments or medals. Typically, Ghiberti's bronze *St. Matthew* was commissioned by the Banker's Guild in 1419 and supervised by four consuls of the Guild, among them Cosimo de' Medici.

Figure 12

Figure 13

Figure 14

Figure 15

PART III   DEVELOPMENTS IN FLORENTINE SCULPTURE

(i)   Sculpture, ideology and church furniture

48   Virtually all sculpture during this period was made for some religious, devotional function, was part of the decoration of a specific space or building, and had a 'plot' or at least some moral or narrative content. Sculpture was made for a pulpit, a font, some doors, a singing-gallery, the niches of a façade, a tomb, or an altar-piece. It often had to fit a pre-existing building shape and often formed part of a scheme to which other artists, past and present contributed. Its function had to be recognizable to a mass audience and so, by and large, it followed traditional patterns (like that often dictating that Fonts should tell the story of St. John the Baptist) of church furniture. Now, look at Donatello's *Tomb for Pope John XXIII* 1424–27 (Figure 17) and a reconstruction of the Orso monument made a century earlier for the Cathedral in 1323 (Figure 18). Make short notes on the way you think Donatello's tomb was affected by the context he worked in. Look as well at later tomb designs (*Murray*, Figures 177, 178, 180).

49   When he made this tomb, Donatello used elements traditional to such a form. He had to, because he worked at a time when sculpture was strictly ideological in function and he therefore had to work for a mass audience – the congregation – as well as 'playing to' a very small coterie of intellectuals and fellow sculptors. Both tombs operate on four successive strata and there are similar ingredients: the parted curtains, the tomb proper, the Virgin and Child and the three figures on the base, which are in Donatello's case, the three Christian virtues, Faith, Hope and Charity. There *are* differences of course, and they really represent those things which are new about fifteenth-century sculpture: the classical cherubs holding up an inscription in precise Roman lettering, the classical architectural ornament, and the fact that the Pope's effigy is in bronze. Unlike later sculptors, Donatello had to use these motifs in the cramped space between two massive pillars which were part of the interior structure of the Florentine Baptistry. It is this narrow space which probably explains the way Donatello avoided ornamental clutter, stressed horizontals throughout the design and used the sweeping curve of the shell niche enclosing the Virgin and Child and the draped canopy to soften the outline of those two massive pillars.

50   Now read this description by Piero Cennini in 1475 of what interested him in the final pair of bronze doors made by Ghiberti for the Baptistry (Figure 19). Read Ghiberti's description of the scenes in the panels too. (*Holt*, pp. 160–3). What features interested Cennini in particular? Is there any modern art form which gives you the sort of experience he is describing?

> [Strangers] passing through Florence view them [the doors] eagerly; they are captured by a desire to see, looking carefully at the details and [while] the day slips quietly by. But who would not be captured by the sight of such wonders? Who would not stand transfixed almost out of his mind when confronted with those men of action and these diverse deeds so convincingly rendered?
>
> R. Krautheimer (1956) *Lorenzo Ghiberti*, Oxford University Press, p. 17.

51   Cennini talks as though the spectator could and should become completely engrossed and absorbed for, literally, *hours* looking, or even 'reading' the stories represented on the doors. He likes a strong story-line, packed full of incidents, variety and action. He sees sculpture as captivating and convincing.

He talks of an expérience which I only associate with an evening at the cinema. This comparison, however peculiar it seems, is valid, for sculpture was expected to tell the story of 'men of action', with a strong moral dichotomy running through the plot and lots of sheer entertainment. The ideology behind this was St. Gregory's. He had said that art was 'the book of the illiterate'. Many of the aims of sculpture at this time derive from this statement: the love of intriguing detail, the fascination with varied scenes, emotional impact and sheer story-telling in realistic and convincing terms. There are suggestions for the development of realism in Unit 10 (Part 2 (i)–(iii)). There is one other interesting consequence of the mass, ideological basis of sculpture: that is the status of 'innovation' or the 'avant-garde'. Strictly speaking there was no 'avant-garde' as we know it. Sculpture was a mass art form based on strong religious conventions and the mass audience (the congregation) really seems to have kept pace with change and applauded it.

52   In other words, sculpture was not usually made for a private collector, a gallery or as an *objet d'art*. It did share some of the characteristics of sculpture made for that sort of function: in particular the display of 'taste' and the

Figure 18

'problems' of art mentioned at the end of Part 1, but it also had to point a moral, commemorate an event, decorate a building, entertain and move a congregation, further the political prestige of a guild or a whole commune and fulfil a devotional function. Like the techniques and materials used, this social and religious function was the context in which the sculptor worked. It was not necessarily a 'constraint' on him.

ii)   New types of statuary and relief

53   I have stressed that sculpture in this period was designed to decorate a building or provide church 'furniture' and that its function was social and public rather than private and personal. But the most interesting developments in sculpture at this time do, in fact, show a trend away from the dependence on architecture which had been the rule for large scale sculpture for a thousand years in Europe, and, in some special areas, a trend towards a more private and personal function. The most obvious examples of these trends are, respectively, the creation of large statues in the round like Donatello's *Judith and Holofernes* (Figure 14), his *David* (*Murray*, Figure 31) and his *Gattemelata* (*Murray*, Figure 32); interest in portrait-busts like Rossellino's *Chellini* (Figure 20) and little bronze statuettes like Pollaiuolo's *Hercules and Antaeus* (Figure 21). These three types of sculpture are all Florentine renovations of classical forms.

54   Portrait busts were often modelled on plaster casts, as Vasari describes in Verrocchio's studio.

> Andrea was very fond of making plaster casts, for which he used a soft stone quarried in the districts of Volterra and Siena and in many other parts of Italy. When this stone is baked in the fire, and then crushed and made into a paste with tepid water, it becomes so soft that it can be fashioned into whatever shape is wanted, and then when it has dried out it sets so hard that whole figures can be cast from it. In the moulds he made from this stone Andrea used to cast various natural forms, such as knees, legs, arms, and torsos, which he kept by him for copying purposes. Then, during Andrea's lifetime, the custom started of doing inexpensive casts of the heads of those who died; and so one can see in every house in Florence, over the chimney-pieces, doors, windows, and cornices, endless examples of such portraits, so well made and natural that they seem alive. . . . From Andrea also came the technique of making far more perfect images not only in Florence but also in every centre of devotion where the faithful come in thanksgiving with their votive offerings or 'miracle pictures' as they are called. Formerly these were small and made in silver, or on small painted panels or crudely fashioned in wax; then in Andrea's time a far better style was introduced. What happened was that Andrea was very friendly in Florence with a skilful craftsman in waxwork called Orsino, who started to teach him how to attain perfection in that craft. Then when Giuliano de' Medici was killed and his brother Lorenzo wounded in Santa Maria del Fiore, Lorenzo's friends and relations ordered that, in thanksgiving to God for his preservation, images of him should be set up throughout the city. So for his part Orsino, with the help and advice of Andrea, made three life-size figures in wax with a wooden framework (as I describe elsewhere) completed with split canes and a covering of waxed cloth, folded and arranged so well that the result was wonderfully attractive and lifelike. He then made the heads, hands, and feet, using a coating of thicker wax, copying the features from life, and painting them in oils with the hair and other adornments. The results of this skilful work were so natural that the wax figures seemed real and alive, as can be seen today from the three figures themselves. One of them is in the church of the nuns of Chiarito, in Via di San Gallo, in front of the miraculous crucifix. This statue is dressed exacly as Lorenzo was when, bandaged and wounded at the throat, he stood at the windows of his house and showed himself to the people who had come to see whether, as they hoped, he was alive or whether they would have to avenge his death.

The second of the statues, dressed in the citizen's gown worn in Florence, is in the church of the Servites (the Annunziata) above the lower door by the table where the candles are sold.

Vasari: *The Lives of the Artists*, trans. G. Bull, Penguin, 1965, pp. 239–40.

They were therefore highly realistic. These and the little bronze statuettes were made for a private market and to be displayed largely in a house. This is an important change in patronage in itself. The little bronzes seem to have been first made by followers of Donatello and perhaps derive from the little bronze figures he made for the Font in Siena Cathedral. Designed for a private connoisseur as portable ornaments, they are the closest equivalent of present day gallery, art-market orientated sculpture. No civic or religious significance needed to be imposed on their frankly classical, pagan subjects. Being so small and having no special setting they tend to be more experimental and varied in form than larger scale sculpture. Yet they are freer only because they are so small and are private in function. They would have been thought less 'important' than, say, Donatello's *David* (*Murray*, Figure 31). Typically, the *David* uses classical forms and motifs in terms of a specifically religious theme. The same is true of portrait-busts. They were 'only' displays of realism, not the use of realism to create a religious 'character', like Donatello's prophet *Habbakuk* (Figure 22) with deep moral significance.

55 Still, there is a *caveat*. It is by no means certain that realistic portraiture was *not* regarded as functional in a religious sense at this time. Wax portraiture (from which the fashion of marble and *terracotta* portraiture probably derives) had a strong votive function. The church of *SS. Annunziata* in Florence was filled with hundreds of wax portraits often painted and dressed, and left there in front of the altar by their owners in the primitive and magical belief that they somehow 'represented' them. Vasari's description of Lorenzo's image is especially interesting. Portraiture here has the function of commemoration,

Figure 20

and a protection against further political and personal disaster. So interest in realistic portraiture may have a lot to do with the feeling that the image 'holds' something of what it represents.

EXERCISE

56   Sculpture seems to have become less dependent on architecture and freer from being 'just' part of the decoration of a building as interest in realism and bronze grew. Read the Appendix on Perspective (paragraphs 62–68) and remind yourself of the characteristics of bronze. Then look carefully at the following list of sculptures and suggest connections between the growth of independence in sculpture and the development of interest in realism and bronze as a medium.

St. George: marble statue and relief by Donatello, 1417 (*Murray*, Figures 24, 25)
St. Matthew: bronze, Ghiberti, 1419–21 (*Murray*, Figure 22)
Judith and Holofernes: bronze, Donatello, 1457–60 (Figure 14)
David: bronze, Donatello, 1430–32 (*Murray*, Figure 31)
Gattemelata: bronze, Donatello 1447–53 (*Murray*, Figure 32)
The Feast of Herod: bronze, Donatello, 1423–27 (Figure 23)
The Story of Joseph: bronze, Ghiberti, 1434–53 (*Murray*, Figure 23)
St. Peter receiving the Keys: marble, Donatello, 1425–30 (Figure 2)

DISCUSSION (Diagrammatic summary, Figure 24)

57   Typically the first large figures in-the-round were made in bronze, which you will remember is a much more flexible medium than stone, and allows the sculptor to produce the sort of free and open shapes he needs to provide an all round interest in a figure widely separated from a building. Bronze was increasingly used for relief sculpture too and it meant that the surface of the relief could be articulated in a very complex and varied way. In Donatello's *Feast of Herod* and in Ghiberti's *Story of Joseph* the largest figures are virtually detached from the main surface of the relief, and in general the amount of projection has been subtly varied, depending on the significance of the figures for the story and on the imagined distances represented. Previous relief in stone and bronze had projected relatively little from the surface of the wall or slab on which it rested, or could be read quite simply as projecting figures on a flat ground, like Ghiberti's first bronze door panels (*Murray*, Figures 19, 20). A stone relief set in a stone frame (or a stone statue in a stone niche) produces a much more homogeneous effect than bronze on stone. It is typical that some of the Guilds of Or San Michele and the Cathedral of Siena had each begun by planning, respectively, stone figures for their niches and stone reliefs for their font and had finally chosen bronze which produces an obvious distinction between architecture and sculpture (*Murray*, Figures 22, 24).

58   During this period sculptors became fascinated by two sorts of realism: the realistic space created by perspective lines and foreshortening, and the type of facial and anatomical observation which conveys the expression of emotion in a 'personality' represented. Both types of realism affect the independence of sculpture. Interest in perspective tends to turn the stone or bronze relief into something which is both decoration *and* 'a window in the wall'. The most extreme examples of this are the 'flattened reliefs' produced by Donatello. This relief type creates effects by the manipulation of the most minute projection

Figure 19

Figure 2

Figure 21

Figure 22

on a slab of marble. The highest relief modelling used in *St. Peter receiving the Keys* is only two millimetres deep and is only used for the figure and tree on the right of the scene. For the rest, Donatello has created space and distance by scratching trees and a city in receding perspective. The whole surface of the relief is animated and he uses the chisel almost as a brush. This relief and that representing *St. George and Dragons* aim at pictorial effects, and it is no coincidence that *St. Peter receiving the Keys* was probably made for the altar-piece of the Brancacci chapel whose painted walls you will see in the television programme in Week 13, and was intended to match the paintings in this chapel (*Murray*, Figure 38). This type of relief ultimately attempts to dissolve the surface of the wall and it is typically the first art form (in *St. George and the Dragon* 1417) to show the use of the perspective of Brunelleschi. Instead of decorating the wall or articulating its shape, it contradicts the very tangibility of the architecture.

59   Interest in the other type of realism – the creation of 'personality' in stone or bronze – freed the niche figure from its setting. A medieval sculptor would take delight in echoing the abstract shapes of the architectural setting in his figure, especially, say, in the drapery. A Ghiberti cannot do that. He tries to counterfeit a 'person' standing in a niche. His *St. Matthew* and Donatello's *St. George* are not so much statues as figures telling a whole 'story' in their gestures, pose and facial expression. Their gaze is firmly focused, the twists in their stance contain energy. The sense of alertness and readiness (of 'men of action') which critics called *prontezza* derives from slight but cumulative exaggerations: of the weight of their limbs, the intensity of their frown. These exaggerations which are especially obvious in Donatello's *Habbakuk* (Figure 22) set up the feeling that the figure is about to step out of the niche. Typically, Donatello in his *St. George* pushed all the narrative he couldn't convey in the single figure into the little relief below, where landscape, building, a maiden, a dragon and a house could be specified: filling out the story of the statue above.

60   So, while sculpture was still, in many ways, traditional in organization and function, the development of private patronage, the trend away from dependence on architecture, the fascination with the 'problems' of art all meant that many features of fifteenth-century Florentine sculpture were ultimately at variance with conventional modes of working, and thus represent a significantly 'new' style.

61   In this unit I have concentrated on describing the way in which a study of both techniques and social or religious function, can help you to understand the innovations and traditions of sculpture in this period. The explanation for these sculptors' interest in realism and classicism will be found in suggestions made in Unit 10. I have mentioned the debate about whether the style of the period was a new modern one, or whether it was simply a recreation of something much older, only in so far as it was involved in my argument. In the next unit, Tim Benton will concentrate on this debate as it applies to architecture.

APPENDIX I

Renaissance perspective

62   From the time of Vitruvius (first century A.D.), if not earlier, perspective drawing of various kinds has been repeatedly picked out as one of the most important skills an architect needs in designing a building. Vitruvius (Book I, Chapter II) defines *arrangement* as follows:

> Arrangement includes the putting of things in their proper places and the elegance of effect which is due to adjustments appropriate to the character of the work. Its forms of expression are these: groundplan, elevation, and perspective. . . . Perspective is the method of sketching a front with the sides withdrawing into the background, the lines all meeting in the centre of a circle.
>
> *The Ten Books on Architecture*, trans. M. H. Morgan, 1960, Dover.

If you turn to *Holt* (p. 241), and read from the twelfth line from the bottom to the end of the section (top of p. 243), you'll see what stress Alberti placed on perspective, mathematics and geometry.

63   Perspective is a perfect example of the stress laid by Renaissance artists and architects on science, on all kinds of knowledge. In many ways, perspective in painting corresponds to the study of proportional theory in architecture; both sought to find objective rules, rules derived from geometry and arithmetic, which would reveal a part of nature's secrets and help the architect or artist to make more beautiful works.

64   In the second half of the fifteenth century, the study of perspective theory became more exclusively a mathematical consideration. It came to centre around the problem of finding a mathematical formula which would express, in numerical terms the diminution in size of objects receding into space, allowing for various factors such as the distance of the eye from the picture plane and its height above the ground. This was the sort of thing which Leonardo wanted to solve (see *Holt*, pp. 278–80), and Piero della Francesca liked to tackle extremely difficult exercises in foreshortening (see *Holt*, pp. 253–67). Alberti, on the other hand, in his *Della Pittura* (1435/6) wanted to complete a more elementary task. For him and his contemporaries, perspective was still largely a mystery. His is the pioneer document on perspective, summing up earlier theories, such as Brunelleschi's, and carrying them further.

65   Many painters had already discovered a system of perspective which depended on a horizon line, at eye level, a vanishing point (exactly opposite the eye), in which all the orthogonals (parallel lines running at right angles to the horizon line) met. This is called the centric point system (see Figure A1). They had developed an aid to setting up a perspective scheme, involving a chequered pavement, which could be accurately drawn receding into the distance, before adding the figures and buildings. This chequered pavement was easy enough to construct, because all the parallel lines converged to a point, while all the horizontal lines were parallel to the bottom of the picture plane (see Figure A2). The only difficult part was where to place these

horizontals. A rule of thumb had been developed by which, after placing the first line by eye, you added the others by cumulatively subdividing the intervals by two-thirds, down to the point where the intervals were too small. The rate of diminution was quite effective, but the random placing of the first horizontal made the whole thing too variable. The higher you placed this line, the greater the apparent distortion.

66   What Alberti did was to remove much of this rule-of-thumb attitude and substitute a theory of vision and a series of steps which amounted to creating a three-dimensional effect from logically combining an elevation with a ground plan. The crucial additionally controlled factor was the distance of the eye from the picture and its height from the ground. In other words, he made it possible to control the viewpoint; the artist could decide whether the spectator was going to 'see' the scene from close to or far away. In a cruder way, this is what Brunelleschi was after with his perspective panels (see the television programme and Figure A5). He could control the viewpoint by fixing it in the peephole in the back of the picture itself. But Alberti controlled the viewpoint through the perspective alone.

67   We can't run through all the steps he advocated, which are quite complicated, but the points to remember are these: Alberti was primarily interested in the simple squared pavement as a means of 'transferring' diminution to the figures. That is, he would begin his picture with such a squared pavement (see Figure A3) and use it as a diminution grid, from which he could read off how high a figure should be standing on any particular square. Secondly, to make this grid more deliberately scaled to the figures who would stand on it, he made the pavement squares equal to the third of a man's height (one Florentine *braccio*). Thirdly, his theory of vision, taken over from ancient and medieval optics, substituted for the visual cone mentioned by earlier writers, the concept of a visual pyramid. Earlier writers had defined sight in terms of straight rays of light which could be conceived as a cone, with the apex in the eye. But Alberti's pyramid made the connection explicit between this and the rectangular picture frame. A painting could be thought of as an end-on view of the visual pyramid, from where the eye of the painter was, and the painting itself would be an intersection of this pyramid (see Figure A4: a b c d). In Alberti's system, the painting was a diminution of the final intersection of the picture plane, which occurred at the point where the scene to be represented started, and which extended vertically above the ground. It was this plane which he used to work out the diminution of the horizontals (see Figure A4). Don't worry if the construction and diagrams appear rather complicated. The key point to grasp is that Alberti arrived at his perspective schemes by drawing what were in fact diagrams of the scene itself and the artist's relationship with them, and simply drawing straight lines between objects or points in the elevation diagram which intersected the perspective plane, which was itself in scale with the painting. Therefore these intersection points could simply be transferred onto the picture surface. Thus, a statue on a pedestal (PQ) could be drawn in elevation on one diagram and located precisely on the perspective drawing by marking off the intersection point (x) on the perspective plane and transferring it to the same height in the picture.

68   As a result of Alberti's findings, it is possible to draw ground plans and elevations of many Renaissance paintings; in some cases this reveals fascinating new levels of interpretation. What principally emerges from a study of Alberti's perspective theory is that it is supremely practical. It allows the artist great flexibility in placing the horizon line, vanishing point and all the figures in the painted scene. Above all, it introduced a new standard of realism, because the perspective plane always began at ground level and the whole system was related to

the human scale, that of a man standing at the front of the picture space. Alberti stressed that the picture was a window, or a transparent veil through which the imagined space was seen, but there is also the idea of a transparent wall through which the artist imagined he could walk directly into the picture space. This illusion was achieved without considerations of the actual size of the picture, provided that the eye is positioned at the right distance from it. Piero della Francesca's *Flagellation*, which is our front cover illustration, is a perfect example of Albertian perspective.

Figure 24
A good example of the effect of techniques described in paragraph 36.

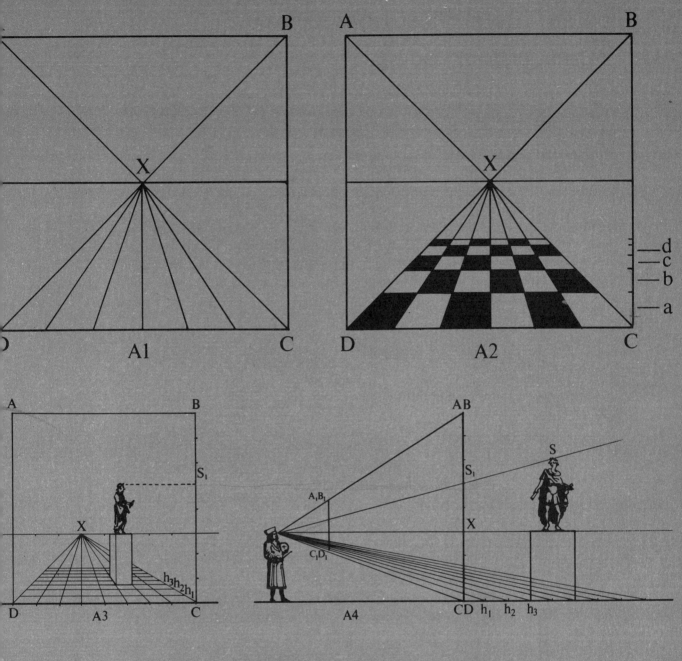

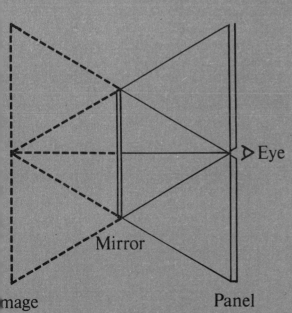

Figures A 1–5
A1 shows the simplest kind of vanishing point perspective. The orthogonals are lines parallel to the line of sight in real space but are seen as converging on a vanishing point in perspective like railway lines. A2 illustrates the way converging orthogonals were used to create a simple 'stage' on which the action could be represented. In this diagram, the gaps between the horizontals diminish by two-thirds; the intervals are marked up the right-hand side of the 'picture' ($a: b = b: c = c: d = 3: 2$). A3 shows the finished picture using Alberti's method. The horizontal lines and the height of the raised statue are arrived at by constructing diagram A4, which is a sideways view of the artist and the scene he is supposed to be painting, divided by a plane (ABCD) which represents the cross-section of the visual pyramid of which the painting is a copy. The distance of the artist (or the spectator) is crucial to the result. From the artist's eye, lines are drawn to the points marking the horizontals of the squares (h^1, h^2, h^3, etc.), and where these lines cross the base of the visual pyramid (ABCD), they establish the intervals to be marked off on A3. Any other points, plotted in elevation in A4 (like the statue's head intersecting ABCD at S_1), can be transferred to A3 in the same way (S_1). A5: a diagram of Brunelleschi's method of demonstrating his perspective panels, using a mirror to compare the painted image with the scene represented. This experiment was demonstrated in the television programme for Unit 9. Figure 51 represents precisely the view seen by Brunelleschi and filmed in the television programme.

35

UNIT 9   THE CONTRIBUTIONS MADE BY BRUNELLESCHI AND ALBERTI TO A NEW STYLE IN THE ANTIQUE MANNER

69   This unit contains two strands, treated in a different way, and covering different ground. Brunelleschi will be taught primarily by Howard Burns, who has written Part II, as well as the radio and television programmes. Alberti will be taught from a reading of *Wittkower* and from an investigation of Alberti's architectural theory and practice. It is important to try to see and hear the two programmes for this week, and time your work on Part II to coincide with this. Please try to make the maximum use of the illustrations and the notes which accompany them, printed in Appendix II.

Contents

Part I   A survey of the sources of fifteenth-century architecture, including a glossary of architectural terms

Part II   Brunelleschi's architecture

Part III   A commentary to Wittkower's *Architectural Principles in the age of Humanism*, selected passages from which will be read at this point

Part IV   Alberti's architectural theory in *De Re Aedificatoria*

Part V   Alberti's architecture, in the light of Part IV

Part VI   Conclusions on architectural theory and practice and the Florentine Renaissance

You may need to refer to Appendix I, printed at the end of Unit 8, and Appendix II contains valuable information on the buildings illustrated in the text.

Figures for Unit 9

Unless otherwise credited, all photographs are by Tim Benton. The author would like to thank John Taylor for his help with the art work.

25   Chartres Cathedral, interior (*Mansell Collection*).
26   Florence Cathedral, interior.
27   SS. Apostoli, interior.
28   S. Lorenzo, interior.
29   Loggia dei Lanzi (*Mansell Collection*).
30   S. Miniato al Monte, façade (*Mansell Collection*).
31   Loggia degli Innocenti.
32   S. Maria Novella, façade.
33   Loggia dei Lanzi, capital.
34   S. Maria Novella, capital in interior.
35   S. Lorenzo, capital in interior.
36   Florence Baptistry, capital on exterior.
37   Corinthian order from Vignola, numbered for glossary.
38   Cupola of Florence Cathedral, cross-section.
39   S. Lorenzo, view across the crossing to south transept.

40   S. Lorenzo, one bay.
41   Old Sacristy, interior.
42   Pazzi Chapel, interior.
43   S. Spirito, view of corner between north transept and aisle.
44   S. Spirito, one bay.
45   S. Maria degli Angeli, plan.
46   S. Spirito, plan.
47   Exedra at the base of the drum of Florence Cathedral.
48   S. Trinità, plan.
49   S. Lorenzo, plan.
50   Donatello tondo relief, from the Old Sacristy (*Howard Burns*).
51   Florence Baptistry.
52   Inside the twin shell of the cupola, Florence Cathedral.
53   Inside the twin shell of the cupola of the Baptistry.
54   Old Sacristy, capital (*Howard Burns*).
55   Capital from Giotto's *Ascension of the Evangelist*, Peruzzi Chapel, S. Croce (*Uffizi*).
56   Pantheon, Rome, capital from the portico.
57   Old Sacristy, plan.
58   Church of Castiglione d'Olona, plan.
59   Holy Sepulchre in the Rucellai chapel, lantern.
60   Lantern originally on the Old Sacristy.
61   Baptistry of Padua Cathedral, plan.
62   Taddeo Gaddi, *Presentation of the Virgin* (detail), Baroncelli Chapel, S. Croce (*Mansell Collection*).
63   Vitruvius's intercolumniations.
64   Three of the five orders, from Vignola.
65   S. Pancrazio, portico.
66   Vitruvian temple.
67   Vitruvius's version of the Etruscan temple.
68   Alberti's version of the Etruscan temple.
69   Plan of S. Andrea, Mantua.
70   Basilica of Maxentius.
71   Reconstruction of the Basilica of Maxentius.
72   Palazzo Rucellai, façade.
73   Palazzo Rucellai, Corinthian capital.
74   S. Maria Novella, capital from the façade.
75   Palladio's Doric capital, *The Four Books of Architecture*.
76   A comparison between the Doric of the Palazzo Rucellai and the Doric order as described in Alberti's *De Re Aedificatoria*.
77   S. Maria Novella, diagram 1.
78   S. Maria Novella, diagram 2.
79   S. Maria Novella, diagram 3.
80   S. Francesco, Rimini, diagram.
81   Pantheon, Rome, cross-section.
82   Drawing of Matteo de' Pasti's medal of Alberti's design for S. Francesco, Rimini, 1450.
83   SS. Annunziata, plan.
84   Triumphal Arch, from *De Re Aedificatoria*.
85   Roman theatre, from *De Re Aedificatoria*.
86   Palazzo Venezia, Rome.

PART I   THE SOURCES OF FIFTEENTH-CENTURY ARCHITECTURE

70   It is impossible in a few pages to give an adequate idea of the stylistic characteristics which mark Renaissance architecture. My aim in Part I is merely to draw your attention to some of the more clear-cut differences between the architecture of the Renaissance and what went before. I want to make two distinctions, first, between what we know as Gothic architecture and pre-Renaissance Italian architecture, and, secondly, between Italian pre-Renaissance architecture and the architecture of Brunelleschi and Alberti. If you find this very baffling, you might like to look at a survey of Renaissance architecture in Peter Murray (op. cit.). For these exercises, you may find the notes in Appendix II helpful.

EXERCISE 1

Look at the church interiors in Figures 25–28. The first is a Gothic building, the last is a Renaissance building. List in your notebook the features in Figures 26 and 27 which appear to you to be similar to Figures 25 and 28, in separate columns.

SPECIMEN ANSWER

Features similar to Figure 25	Figure 28
In Figure 26: Pointed arches in the walls and ceiling *Ribs*[1] supporting the ceiling *Compound piers* which are divided into *shafts* to correspond with the *ribs* A strong vertical emphasis	*In Figure 26:* Relative simplicity in wall and ceiling surfaces Round windows, though differently placed
In Figure 27: No significant ones	*In Figure 27:* Round arches *Columns* with a single *capital* on each Chapels in the side walls Great simplicity of detail A horizontal emphasis

EXERCISE 2

Look at the façades in Figures 29–32. Figures 29 and 31 are 'Loggias', placed like a porch before a building as a sort of open-air vestibule. The other two are church façades. List the features (a) which each pair (Figures 29 and 31 and Figures 30 and 32) have in common and (b) which are different between each pair.

[1]Italicized words in this section are explained in the glossary (p. 46).

Figure 25

Figure 2

Figure 27

Figure 2

Figure 29

Figure 30

Figure 31

Figure 32

SPECIMEN ANSWER

Features in common	Differences
Figures 29 and 31 Round-headed arches on the outside, *corbels* (*capitals* without *columns*) fixed to the wall inside	*Figures 29 and 31* The supports for the arches in Figure 29 are *compound piers* The supports in Figure 31 are *columns*
Figures 30 and 32 Surface decoration in both is achieved with a pattern of dark lines on white Both have triangular *pediments* Both have round-headed arches applied to the wall on the lower storey Both have *pilasters* on the upper storey Both are quite highly decorated but appear clear and fairly logical in their ornament	Figure 29 has Gothic detailing: the parapet, the *capitals*, the niches Figure 31 is more graceful, lighter in feeling *Figures 30 and 32* Figure 32 has an *attic* The round-headed arches in Figure 32 are long and thin and rest on long *pilasters* instead of *half-columns*, as in Figure 30 The *columns* in Figure 32 extend right up to the entablature, instead of to the supporting arches, as in Figure 30 Figure 32 has a round window in the upper storey

EXERCISE 3

Look at the architectural details in Figures 33–36. The first two are unclassical in various ways, while the other two are more classical.

A   Referring to the diagram of three of the classical *orders* (Figure 64) and to the glossary (p. 46), list the features in Figures 33 and 34 which appear to you to be classical and unclassical.

B (i)   What is classical about Figures 35 and 36?

  (ii)   What differences are there between these two and the Corinthian *order* in Figure 37?

 (iii)   What differences are there between the *capitals* in Figures 35 and 36?

Figure 33

Figure 34

Figure 35

Figure 36

A   SPECIMEN ANSWER

Unclassical features	Classical features
Figure 33 The capital, although remotely like a *Corinthian* capital, has very different foliage The *capital* is divided up into vertical sections to correspond with the *shafts* and *ribs* The *pier* is a *compound pier* The niches containing the relief statues of the Virtues, based on a triangle and semicircles, are unclassical *Figure 34* The *capital* is still composed of three vertical elements to correspond with the *ribs* The *ribs* are decorated with unclassical abstract ornaments	*Figure 33* Immediately above the *capital*, is a strip which looks like a simplified version of a classical *entablature* Although the *capital* is divided into strips, the effect of foliage is to unite the *capital* into one big one *Figure 34* This *capital* is a Gothic paraphrase of a classical *Corinthian capital*. Although the foliage is not 'correct', the general layout of the leaves is right and so is the underlying form of the *abacus*, with projections at the corners The main part of the *pier* is *semi-circular* in section, like a classical *half-column*

B   SPECIMEN ANSWER AND DISCUSSION

These features, at least, should be obvious:

1   The *volutes*, the two rows of *acanthus* (or olive) leaves around the main part, the *abacus* with its concave sides and the *flower* in the middle of each side and the convex lip of the *vase* counteracting it. They also share the *architrave* with superimposed layers of stone, surmounted by a form of *frieze* and topped by a *cornice*, though there are differences in detail between them.

2   You may have spotted that in both Figures 35 and 36, the whole *entablature* is chopped up into a block which extends only over the capital. From the top of this *entablature* spring arches. In a normal classical arrangement, the *entablature* would continue to the next column and would itself support the wall above, without any arches (cf. Figure 66).

3   Differences between Figures 35 and 36: Figure 35 is more sculptural and bolder, the *volutes* are all of equal size, instead of making the middle ones smaller as they should be, the *frieze* in Figure 35 is decorated with relief sculpture, as are the arches. The whole *entablature* has been elongated in height to make it more visible from the ground. In Figure 36, the details of the *entablature* are treated rather skimpily, especially the cornice. The *column shaft* has been faced (at a later date) with dark and light panels of marble.

If you didn't get most of these, look again at the illustrations and check them. There are many other points you could have made, but these are the most obvious ones. One thing should be clear; identifying classical features in a building involves looking very closely at particular details and comparing these with classical prototypes.

71   If you look back at these exercises and look again at the notes to the figures, it should be clear that the vestiges of the classical style survived in Italian architecture better than in the North. Round arches were often used in Florence in the Middle Ages, and Gothic piers and capitals were quite close at times to classical prototypes. Some buildings, like S. Miniato and SS. Apostoli, provided close models for Renaissance architects to follow. In this way, we can say that the Renaissance architects learned a great deal from the Italian architecture that went before, which it could not have learnt from, say, Chartres Cathedral.

72   On the other hand, we must insist that Brunelleschi and Alberti made innovations which went beyond any previous efforts to revive the antique style. It is possible to use the architectural terminology of antiquity to describe the details of Renaissance architecture, whatever minor differences there may be, while Gothic detailing needs different terms to describe it. The rules of antique architecture were never completely unalterable, but there was a definite 'language' with precise conventions and this language and these conventions began to be assimilated during the Renaissance. As we will see, however, this is not the only way in which one can describe Renaissance architecture; Brunelleschi and Alberti contributed much more to architectural history than a few fairly exact copies from surviving fragments of antique detailing.

73   Finally, to test whether you have got the 'feel' of the differences between earlier Italian architecture and that of the Renaissance, look again at Figure 32. Part of this façade was built in the fourteenth century, part was only finished in 1470. See if you can spot which parts are early and which are late. You'll find out the answers later in the unit (paragraph 127). It isn't an easy task.

GLOSSARY

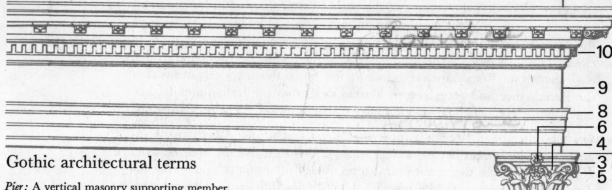

- 10
- 9
- 8
- 6
- 4
- 3
- 5
- 2

Gothic architectural terms

Pier: A vertical masonry supporting member.

Compound pier: A pier with several elements (shafts) running up it, each of which appear to support a *rib* or arch.

Rib: A strip of strengthened masonry which helps to support a vaulted ceiling.

Classical terms

Column: Like a pier, but with a circular section, with prescribed proportions and with a slight taper towards the top. A row of free-standing columns supporting an *entablature* is called a *colonnade.*

Half-column: A column applied to a wall, with semi-circular section.

Pilaster: Like a half-column, but rectangular in section and usually projecting only slightly from the wall.

These forms should conform with one of the five classical *orders* (Figure 64), in proportion and detail.

1 *Shaft:* The main part of a column.

2 *Capital:* The decorated block crowning the column. There are Gothic forms for capitals as well as classical, but classical capitals were designed according to the conventional forms of the *orders.*

3 *Abacus:* The top part of the capital.

4 *Vase:* The smooth, lipped core to which the leaves and volutes are 'applied' on the *capital.*

5 *Volutes:* Spiral scrolls emerging from the acanthus leaves on the Corinthian *capital.* Larger volutes were the feature of Ionic capitals (Figure 64).

6 *Flower:* The little flower which decorates the centre of each side of the *abacus* on the Corinthian capital.

7 *Entablature:* The whole horizontal member supported by the columns.

8 *Architrave:* The lowest band of the *entablature,* composed of one or more elements (three in the Corinthian order).

9 *Frieze:* Sometimes left plain, but often decorated; the middle component of the *entablature.*

10 *Cornice:* The top member of the entablature, projecting well away from it, designed to throw off water and protect the entablature.

11 *Base:* The base transferred the weight of the column to the ground, and its convex and concave mouldings gave the impression of powerful compression. The design varied according to the *order.* In Roman architecture, the base was considered essential.

12 *Pedestal:* Used to raise columns from the ground if necessary. Not an essential part of the orders.

Attic: A storey or strip coming above the entablature. Usually occurs at the top of a building, but can be found separating two storeys.

Pediment: The crowning feature of the classical temple; it is a low triangular gable with an *architrave* moulding running along all three sides.

Order: The orders prescribe the details for *columns, capitals, entablatures* and *bases* according to five 'styles', the Tuscan, Doric, Ionic, Corinthian and Composite. Three of these *orders* are illustrated in Figure 64. There was enough variety in antique architecture to make it difficult for architects in the Renaissance to agree exactly on every detail of the *orders.* Alberti stipulated one set of rules, though he never insisted on a blind observance of his rules, but by the end of the sixteenth century, many of his examples had been abandoned in favour of a consensus agreement to adopt those antique examples chosen by Vignola and Palladio.

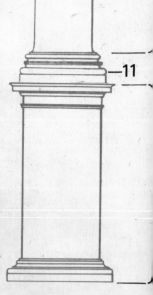

- 11

Figure 37

PART II   BRUNELLESCHI'S ARCHITECTURE

Fillipo Brunelleschi (1377–1446) was, together with Masaccio, Donatello, Ghiberti and Alberti, one of the creators of Renaissance art. Through his invention of perspective, he had an enormous influence on the development of the visual arts in general. He was responsible for the greatest feat of structural engineering since antiquity, the construction of the huge cupola of the Cathedral in Florence. And, more or less single-handed, he invented Renaissance architecture and established a new approach to architectural design which has been followed right up to the present time.

Chronology of Brunelleschi's life and works

1367   Brunelleschi's father, the notary Ser Brunellescho Lippi, voted in the 'referendum' on the design to be followed for the Cathedral, expressing approval for the winning project.

1377   Brunelleschi born in Florence.

1398   Brunelleschi joined the Silk Guild (Arte della Seta), which included the goldsmiths, the profession he had chosen.

1401   Brunelleschi was the runner-up in the competition for the north doors of the Baptistry. The competition reliefs of Ghiberti and Brunelleschi are still preserved (cf. *Holt*, Figures 16 and 17).

1404   Brunelleschi and Ghiberti were members of a committee set up to consider a problem arising in connection with the buttresses of the arms of the crossing of the Cathedral. Brunelleschi was enrolled as a Master in the Arte della Seta, having served his apprenticeship as a goldsmith.

1409   Brunelleschi and some friends played the famous practical joke in which they persuaded a fat carpenter that he was someone else, a debtor called Matteo. This story, recounted in a much read novellette (the *Novella of the Fat Carpenter*) did as much as anything to make Brunelleschi famous.

c. 1414   The drum of the Cathedral was completed, thus rendering immediate the problem, which Brunelleschi was to solve between 1418 and 1420, of how the dome itself could be constructed with so vast a span and at such a height above the ground.

1418   Projects were requested for the construction of the cupola.

1419   Work began, after Brunelleschi's design, on the Ospedale degli Innocenti (Figure 31).

1420   Brunelleschi's programme for the construction of the cupola was accepted. Its construction remained his principal concern until 1436 (Figures 38, 53).

1421   Beginning of work at S. Lorenzo (Figures 28, 35, 39 and 40) and in the Old Sacristy (Figures 41 and 57).

1423   Birth of Brunelleschi's biographer, Manetti.

1425   May and June. Brunelleschi served a term as one of the Priori (i.e. a member of the Florentine government).

1429   The death of Giovanni de' Medici (who had paid for the Old Sacristy) and the completion of the Old Sacristy (though still without Donatello's reliefs and decoration).

1429–30   Work began on the Pazzi Chapel (Figure 42) to Brunelleschi's design.

1430   Brunelleschi was engaged as an adviser at the siege of Lucca.

1434–37   Design and beginning of work on the round church of S. Maria degli Angeli (Figure 45).

1434–6   Brunelleschi made the model for S. Spirito (Figures 43, 44 and 46).

1436   The cupola completed.
Alberti dedicated the Italian version of his book on painting (*Della Pittura*), to Brunelleschi (cf. *Holt*, p. 205).

1439   Decision to construct the four exedrae at the base of the Cathedral cupola after Brunelleschi's model (Figure 47).

1441   Battle of Anghiari, a great Florentine victory over a formidable alliance dominated by the Milanese.

1442   Work at S. Lorenzo, which had stopped in 1429, restarted, paid for by Cosimo de' Medici. The pace of construction speeded up at the Pazzi Chapel.

1446   March   The foundation stone of the lantern of the cupola laid.
       5 April   The first column was raised at S. Spirito.
       15 April   Brunelleschi died.

1461   Completion of the dome over the portico of the Pazzi Chapel, whose main structure was thereby completed.

c. 1470   Completion of S. Lorenzo.

1475   Birth of Michelangelo.

1480s   Manetti's *Life of Brunelleschi* written.

c. 1487   Completion of S. Spirito.

1497   Death of Manetti.

EXERCISE

Divide Brunelleschi's buildings (apart from the cupola) into two groups, those designed before 1430 and those designed after 1434. What are the chief stylistic differences that strike you between these two groups of works?

DISCUSSION

75   Though Brunelleschi's style remains remarkably uniform (much more so than Alberti's), there is a clear difference of approach between the earlier and the later works. In the earlier designs he used flat walls, articulated with pilasters (for instance, S. Lorenzo, Figures 28, 35, 39 and 40). In his later works he mostly used curving walls, with half-columns applied to them, producing a much more moulded and sculptural effect (for instance, S. Spirito, Figures 43, 44 and 46).

76   The chronology of the execution of Brunelleschi's works follows patterns determined by the state of the Florentine economy and, to a lesser extent, the political situation. After a decade of building activity (1419–29), war and political upheavals slowed down progress on the Pazzi Chapel, stopped building at S. Lorenzo, and S. Spirito got off to such a slow start that only one column was standing nine years after the laying of the foundation stone. Economic and political stability returned in the early 1440s (see chronology, 1441, Battle of Anghiari). In 1442, Cosimo made over the income from 40,000 florins for the construction of S. Lorenzo, and Andrea Pazzi followed suit by increasing his grant for the building of the Pazzi Chapel.

77   As can be seen from the chronology, Brunelleschi's ecclesiastical works were completed rather slowly. Only the Cathedral cupola (without the lantern) and the Old Sacristy were finished during Brunelleschi's lifetime and according to his wishes. All his other works, to a greater or lesser extent, were altered in execution. For instance, the side chapels at S. Lorenzo were cut down in size for reasons of economy, and later architects left their mark in other ways at S. Lorenzo after his death. At the Innocenti and in the Old Sacristy, Brunelleschi lived to see his designs altered. Then, with the passage of time (combined with the fact that Brunelleschi often dispensed with committing his ideas to paper or to a model), it often happened that no one could remember what Brunelleschi had intended. This emerges clearly from the minutes of the discussions as to how S. Spirito should be completed.

78   On the whole, medieval architecture was a collective enterprise, and the great Italian churches of the fourteenth and fifteenth centuries were designed by committees. In the execution, individual masons were also given con-

48

siderable freedom to vary the designs in matters of detail and decoration. Brunelleschi represents a new kind of figure on the architectural scene. He was an architect who made himself responsible for the design, and supervision of the execution, of every aspect of the building, whether decorative or structural. This emerges from the whole history of Brunelleschi's direction of the erection of the cupola. Manetti says, for instance, that Brunelleschi liked to inspect personally every brick and stone before it was put into the building. From Manetti's account of his anger at the additions made without his consent at the Old Sacristy and the Innocenti, and from the Innocenti building accounts themselves, it is clear that every detail was designed by Brunelleschi himself. An examination of his buildings further demonstrates the absolute control which he exercised over their design. Every detail is a standardized unit, with no variations allowed. Indeed, so revolutionary was this new concept of the architect's role, that it was not until the sixteenth century that the architect of the Brunelleschian type became the norm in Italy.

eg Manetti exaggeration

79   Wait until you have seen and heard the television and radio programmes for this week before doing this exercise and continuing with Part II. If you want to get on in the meantime, move on to Part III.

EXERCISE

What were Brunelleschi's main contributions to Renaissance art and architecture? Set down your answer in your notebook under three or four headings.

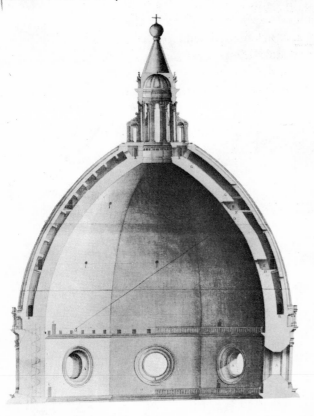

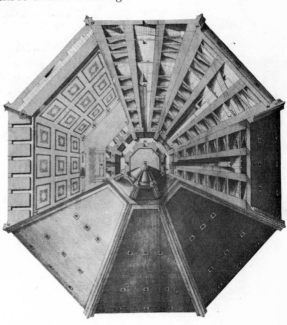

Figure 38

SPECIMEN ANSWER

You should have put something down under the following headings (not necessarily in this order).

1   Brunelleschi was a new type of architect. — *ie detail, new concepts.*
2   The invention of modern perspective.
3   Brunelleschi's use of a classical architectural language.
4   Brunelleschi's development of rational architectural design.

Figure 40

Figure 39

Figure 41

Figure 42

Figure 43

Figure 44

Figure 47

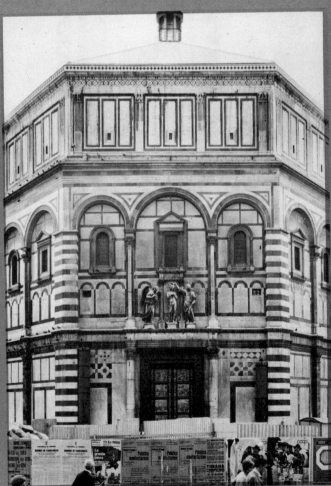

Figure 51

DISCUSSION

1 You should have noted down the main points outlined in paragraph 78. If you didn't, look it through again.

2 Brunelleschi's demonstration of the application of his perspective system, the basis of all modern perspective theory and practice, is described at length by Manetti (cf. *Holt*, pp. 170–3) and analysed by John White (op. cit., see paragraph 9). In the television programme, I demonstrated the method Brunelleschi used to display his perspective discoveries. This system, which is still in use today but which was unknown before Brunelleschi invented it, provided for the convergence of parallel lines on a vanishing point at eye level. Brunelleschi almost certainly provided a rule for dealing with the representation of equally spaced parallel lines receding into the distance in the manner of sleepers on a railway line. Brunelleschi's system was quickly applied and elaborated in theory and practice in the early 1420s by Masaccio (in the fresco of the *Trinity* in S. Maria Novella),[1] by Donatello in the Siena Baptistry relief (see Figure 23) and in the 1430s by Ghiberti in the second gates of the Florentine Baptistry. Alberti set it down in writing and probably elaborated it in his *Della Pittura* (1435 and 1436). An account of Alberti's formulation is contained in Appendix I. Brunelleschian perspective had an immense importance for the whole subsequent development of the visual arts, as well as greatly increasing the possibilities of conveying complicated information in graphic form (as for example in Leonardo's architectural drawings, cf. *Wittkower*, Plates 5a and 5b).

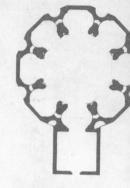

Figure 45

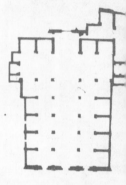

Figure 48

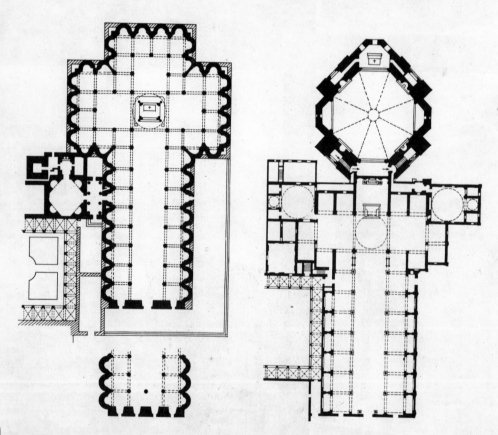

Figures 46 and 49

3 The new type of architectural detail which Brunelleschi introduced, broadly based on that of ancient Roman architecture, became the basis of architectural language throughout the Renaissance and right into the last century.

[1] See Plate 5.

4   More important than Brunelleschi's use of classical detail was the way in which it was used. Brunelleschi's use of capitals, bases and the other parts of the orders is not arbitrary or fanciful but tells a story about structure, even though this story is not always strictly true. Pilasters, for instance, are merely strips of stone veneer applied to the wall and hence only have the air of supporting what is above them – nothing would fall if they were stripped away. This use of classical architectural vocabulary as an explanation of structure remained a feature of much Renaissance architecture. Finally, lighting, layout and decoration are simple, rational and contribute to a unified aesthetic effect. The buildings are perfectly adapted to their function, whether religious, as at S. Spirito, or secular, as at the Innocenti. Brunelleschi's buildings, even in their functional aspect, set new standards. At the Innocenti, for instance, built as a home for abandoned children, Brunelleschi designed, not only the Loggia, but a whole carefully planned complex round a central courtyard, with a chapel, dormitories, kitchens, a refectory and offices for administration.

utilitas

80   Brunelleschi was popularly known in his own time, and throughout the fifteenth century, as the builder of the cupola and the author of the famous practical joke on the fat carpenter. But among artists, the Florentine social and political establishment and the educated élite, he was remembered for his invention of perspective and for his creation of a new architectural style, which was seen as a revival of ancient Roman architecture. Thus there is considerable evidence from his contemporaries to support the evaluation modern architectural historians have made of Brunelleschi's achievement.

81   Giovanni Rucellai, in his private notebook, jotted down some observations on those he considered the four most notable Florentines who had lived in his time. Of Brunelleschi, one of the four, he says:

> Filippo di Ser Brunellescho, of whom it was said that from the time when the Romans lorded it over the world there was no more notable man in architecture than he and expert in geometry and a perfect master of sculpture, and in such things he had great genius and fantasy, and the ancient manner of building in the Roman style was refound by him.
>
> (quoted in Radio Programme 9, trans. Howard Burns.)

Figure 50

53

Giovanni Rucellai's comment is particularly interesting in that, after Cosimo de' Medici, he was the most important Florentine architectural patron of the fifteenth century and had no less than five works built after designs by Alberti, including the façade of his own Palace (cf. Figure 72 and Part V). Interesting, too, is what the Florentine architect Filarete wrote in his architectural treatise in the early 1460s:

> And I bless the soul of Filippo di Ser Brunellescho, famous Florentine citizen and most worthy architect and most subtle imitator of Dedalus, who resuscitated in our city of Florence this ancient manner of building. . . .
>
> (quoted in Radio Programme 9, trans. Howard Burns.)

82 The most notable literary testimony to Brunelleschi's fame is, however, the *Life* which Antonio di Tuccio Manetti wrote of him in the 1480s (op. cit., see paragraph 9). This is the only full length biography of an artist to have been written in the fifteenth century. Manetti himself (1423–97) was an educated silk merchant who occupied a number of important public positions, including a term as head of government in 1495. He also says he had known Brunelleschi and spoken with him. In 1466 he was a member of the Innocenti building committee and in 1491 was called in to advise on the projects for the completion of the Cathedral façade. On this occasion he is described as citizen and architect. His chief reason for writing the *Life* seems to have been the desire to disassociate Brunelleschi from the various errors which had been introduced into his buildings in the course of execution. Manetti in this seems to be simply the most literate spokesman for a whole Brunelleschian party within the Florentine architectural world, which, with only partial success, sought to defend Brunelleschi's projects against those who wanted to alter them.

83 There are other indications of the pro-Brunelleschian current of opinion. In 1457 Giovanni da Guaiuole, who in 1461 became architect in charge at S. Spirito, wrote to Cosimo's son Giovanni, complaining that, after criticizing Manetti's departure from Brunelleschi's model in the cupola at S. Lorenzo, one of Manetti's assistants had attacked him in the street. This Manetti, the architect in charge at San Lorenzo in the 1450s, is not to be confused with Brunelleschi's biographer, who was highly critical of him. In 1486 Giuliano da Sangallo, the leading Florentine architect of his time, made a last minute attempt to get Lorenzo de' Medici to reverse the decision to abandon Brunelleschi's four door solution for S. Spirito in favour of the more conventional but less harmonious three door solution, which in fact was built. Giuliano's letter to Lorenzo reads, in its urgency, like a telegram. Giuliano da Sangallo also carefully copied some of Brunelleschi's projects into his sketchbooks, and

Figures 52 and 53

it is in great part through these drawings that we know what Brunelleschi wanted S. Maria degli Angeli and S. Spirito to look like.

84 Even if the pro-Brunelleschians were not entirely successful in their attempts to see that Brunelleschi's projects were followed, they did keep alive Brunelleschi's approach to architectural design. Leonardo da Vinci's drawings of centralized buildings (cf. *Wittkower*, Plates 5a and 5b) have as their point of departure Brunelleschi's works and projects, and Michelangelo, the friend of Giuliano da Sangallo, can be seen as the ultimate Florentine adherent of the Brunelleschian tradition, with its overriding concern that a building, from the whole scheme down to the smallest detail, should be a completely harmonious and unified whole.

Figure 54

Figure 55

Figure 56

PART III   WITTKOWER'S *ARCHITECTURAL PRINCIPLES IN THE AGE OF HUMANISM*

85   I hope that eventually you will find the time to read the whole of this book. It makes some challenging and exciting claims for the thoroughness with which Renaissance architects, from Alberti's time onwards, put into practice in their buildings theories which some of them had formulated in their writings. Alberti (1404–72) and Palladio (1508–80) (an architect whose career falls outside our period) both wrote architectural treatises in which they made definite statements about the kinds of proportions which should be used in architecture. Wittkower's main argument is that they actually put these categorical statements into effect in their buildings. Both the written evidence and the evidence to be culled from buildings becomes stronger as the period advances and so Wittkower's argument partly rests on the assumption that what was to be explicit in the sixteenth century was in fact implicit in the fifteenth. For these reasons, you will get more out of the book the more you read.

86   Having said that, I felt it unreasonable to demand that you read the whole book, so I will only expect you to read the following passages:

pp. 1–10 (I suggest you read quickly through pp. 11–26).

pp. 27–32.

pp. 33–56.

pp. 101–13 (This section is not absolutely necessary, but will, I think, make the next more understandable).

pp. 113–20.

Appendix I   This is of interest as the purest available example of a Renaissance author explaining the reasons for a proportional system and its thoroughness in execution.

Appendix II This is essential reading, since it expresses the debate over Wittkower's ideas succinctly.

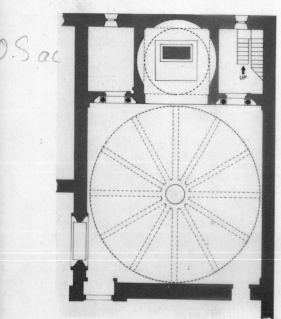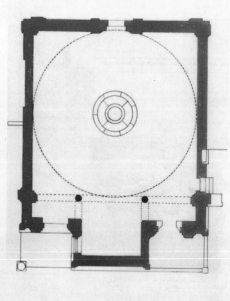

Figures 57 and 61

Vitruvius

37 Wittkower's ideas are far-reaching and complex; we cannot do justice to them here. The key idea I want you to take away is that Renaissance architects were preoccupied with extremely grand, 'philosophical' ideas. The grandeur and breadth of these ideas helps to explain the extent to which architectural thinking and practice developed in the fifteenth century.

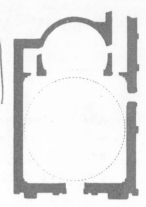

38 I will be dealing with Alberti's architectural theory in Part IV. But as you read the passages indicated above, I want you to look out for the following points and make notes about Wittkower's answers to the following questions:

  1 Why were Renaissance architects interested in geometrical shapes such as the circle and square?

  2 Why would an architect such as Alberti make explicit statements about those proportions an architect should use?

  3 To what extent, in the buildings he designed, was Alberti bound by (a) his proportional theories, and (b) his devotion to the architecture of antiquity?

Figure 58

39 The answers to these questions will emerge from the remainder of the unit, but I hope you will note down the points which emerge from reading Wittkower and which seem to you to answer these questions. Don't skip the footnotes; many of them contain crucial arguments and sometimes contain revisions of Wittkower's central points.

40 When you come to the passages on Alberti's architecture, make sure you refer continually to the illustrations in this unit as well as those in the book. You will find the notes to the illustrations in Appendix II of interest.

Figure 59

Figures 60 and 62

PART IV   ALBERTI AS A THEORIST

91 Alberti's career was very different to Brunelleschi's, and the differences tell us something immediately about their architecture and architectural ideas. Read *Holt*, pp. 203–5.

EXERCISE

Comparing this information with what you know about Brunelleschi's life, what conclusions would you draw about their careers as practising architects, and theorists?

DISCUSSION

Alberti was primarily a humanist scholar who made a living as an ecclesiastical jurist and civil servant. Brunelleschi was trained as a goldsmith. Alberti wrote his *De Re Aedificatoria* before designing most of his best known works. Brunelleschi also came late to architecture, as far as we can tell from the scanty evidence about his early life, but the development from a training as a sculptor, artist or goldsmith to a practice in architecture was typical of the fifteenth and fourteenth centuries. Alberti's career, as far as we can tell, is unusual for the period.

92 Carrying the name, but not the wealth or position, of the Albertis, Leon Battista was not quite a dilettante architect, but was not a professional craftsman either. His fame and prestige as a scholar, author of works on ethics, politics, religion, cartography, mathematics, painting, sculpture and architecture gave him a very special relationship with the patrons of his day, such as Pope Nicholas V, Sigismondo Malatesta of Rimini, Lodovico Gonzaga of Mantua and Giovanni Rucellai of Florence, who commissioned his architectural works. He was intimate with many of the most brilliant humanist minds of his day, all over Italy.

93 This comparison should not be exaggerated; Brunelleschi too was received into humanist circles in Rome and Florence. But the fact remains that Brunelleschi's fame rested primarily on the construction of the great dome on the Cathedral in Florence, while Alberti's most lasting influence was through his books. In Part V I will look at his buildings, but here we will tackle his great architectural treatise, *De Re Aedificatoria* (completed 1452).

94 What were Alberti's aims in writing *De Re Aedificatoria*? This is how the Italian scholar, Paolo Portoghesi sums them up in his introduction to the latest, authoritative edition of the treatise (Leon Battista Alberti, *L'Architettura* (*De Re Aedificatoria*), edited by Giovanni Orlandi, Milan, 1966, hereafter referred to as Orlandi).

> The aim, in *De Re Aedificatoria*, of establishing the objective foundations for a universal [architectural] language, would become the central theme in the Roman classicism of Bramante (1444–1514) at a time when the Papal dream was to restore in its totality the prestige of Rome. But Alberti went on to propose a substantially different aim. For he wanted to do more than restore classicism, he wanted to 'improve on the ancients', by combining what he learnt from them with his own rationale.
>
> (Orlandi, p. xv, trans. Tim Benton.)

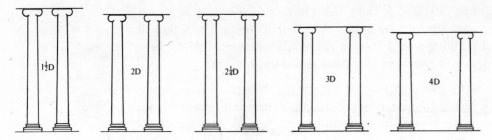

Figure 63

This ambitious aim of Alberti's was only possible because of his immense learning and erudition. He built up his architectural theory from an extraordinarily wide variety of sources, drawing on his work on mathematics, cartography, Platonic and Pythagorean cosmography and musical theory, as well as considerable research into the practical, constructional and utilitarian aspects of building. In this practical sphere, he probably learnt a great deal from his association with Bernardo Rossellino (1409–64), with whom he seems to have collaborated on architectural projects in Rome during the Pontificate of his friend Pope Nicholas V (1447–53).

95   Alberti's aims in *De Re Aedificatoria*, then, were to improve architecture by logical analysis of its function, by reference to the architecture and theory of antiquity, and by reference to all those areas of theoretical speculation which he had mastered. Now let us try to extract from it four major ways in which he wanted to improve the architecture of his day. First, he wanted to interpret the writings of antiquity, particularly Vitruvius's *De Architectura*, and, by extrapolating a set of rules and 'good' principles, show how modern architects could improve their style. Secondly, though this is largely obscured by the first aim, he tried to verify Vitruvius's statements by reference to actual antique building. Thirdly, though in fact this comes first in the structure of *De Re Aedificatoria*, he tried to redefine the function of architecture and codify good common-sense building practice from his vast accumulation of knowledge, including much sound building sense. And fourthly, he tried to formulate some theories of a grander and more far-reaching kind, such as the application of Pythagorean proportional theory to architecture. This last is the kind of formulation which particularly interested Wittkower.

1   The very 'sound rules' of architecture derived from Vitruvius

> From the example of the ancients, from the advice of experts and from continual practice, there is available to us a complete understanding of the methods used in creating these amazing works [the architecture of the Roman Empire]. From this understanding, very sound rules have been deduced, rules which should only be broken, in any way at all, by those who wish to appear incompetent in their buildings – an unlikely ambition. So it is my aim, then, to distinguish these rules and illustrate them to the best of my ability.
>
> Orlandi, Book VI, Chap. III, pp. 456–7, trans. T.B.

96   Many of the 'sound' rules Alberti sets out in *De Re Aedificatoria* come straight from Vitruvius's *De Architectura*. Vitruvius wrote his treatise in the second half of the first century B.C., probably just before 27 B.C. Various manuscripts survived in mutilated form throughout the Middle Ages, but particular interest was revived in 1414 when the humanist Poggio Bracciolini discovered a copy in the Monastery of St. Gall, in Switzerland (cf. Units 5–6, p. 21). It seems

likely that Alberti at first intended to bring out a new critical edition of Vitruvius, but gave it up as too difficult. *De Architectura* is full of obscurities, technical jargon and muddled thinking which had baffled scholars before Alberti's time. Alberti felt that he could improve on Vitruvius and started afresh.

97 What Alberti did was to take over part of Vitruvius's theoretical framework, and in particular, three key Latin words, which both writers thought expressed the qualities necessary for perfection in architecture: *firmitas* (constructional strength), *utilitas* (function, or utility), *venustas* (design or beauty). Unlike Vitruvius himself, Alberti rigidly structured his treatise around these three concepts. Books II and III are mostly about *firmitas*, Books IV and V on *utilitas* and Books VI–IX on *venustas*. The first Book is introductory and the last contains a miscellany of material omitted from the earlier Books.

98 Like Vitruvius, Alberti insisted on wide terms of reference for the architect. The architect must understand what kind of buildings are needed for society (*utilitas*). He must therefore have an understanding of society, of human nature, of what is necessary for man to live his life to the full on the private and public level. In this he went further than Vitruvius. For instance, when describing town planning in Book IV, Chapter I, he felt it necessary to ask first what kind of government was best. Typically, he comes up with a version of Plato's *Republic*, in which the rulers were to be the wisest men, helped by the artistically inclined, while the wealthy would have a much more subservient role than was usual in the governments of his day.

99 There are many ways in which Alberti developed Vitruvius's premisses and material, but he always returned to them, at times quoting from them when

Figure 64

Figure 65

the application to the architecture of his own day must have seemed tenuous. For instance, we can never be certain, in *De Re Aedificatoria*, what is meant by terms such as *templum* which Wittkower claims to be a synonym for *church*, but which Alberti often used to apply to Roman temples. He often described building types such as Roman baths, Roman theatres and Roman triumphal arches as if they were built in his own day. Some of this ambiguity entered into his recommendations for how to tackle everyday architectural problems. For instance, describing intercolumniations (the distance to be left between columns in a colonnade (cf. the glossary, p. 46 under *column*) expressed in terms of the diameter of the column), he followed closely what Vitruvius said in Book III of *De Architectura*. Vitruvius had been describing columns in temple fronts, where one or more rows of columns support a straight entablature (Figure 66). He referred to five proportions for intercolumniations ($1\frac{1}{2}$, 2, $2\frac{1}{4}$, 3 and 4) and selected $2\frac{1}{4}$ as the best (Figure 63). Alberti's recommendations were nearly identical (he substituted $3\frac{3}{8}$ for Vitruvius's 4 for the widest intercolumniation) and yet in Brunelleschi's architecture this ideal proportion of $2\frac{1}{4}$ column-diameters between the columns occurs hardly at all, and seldom enough even in Alberti's buildings.

EXERCISE

See if you can identify an example of an intercolumniation of $2\frac{1}{4}$ column-diameters in the illustrations to this unit. Why are there not more?

DISCUSSION

The closest example is Alberti's portico to the Church of S. Pancrazio (Figure 65). Most of the columns in the illustrations to this unit support arches rather than a straight entablature. Can you imagine what Brunelleschi's *Loggia degli Innocenti* (Figure 31) (with an intercolumniation of at least 4 column-diameters) would look like with an intercolumniation of $2\frac{1}{4}$? Vitruvious condemned wide intercolumniations (such as 4 diameters) on the grounds that stone entablatures would not be strong enough to bridge the wide intervals between the columns. An arch could bridge the gap easily, but architects in Vitruvius's day always placed a straight entablature over columns. Thus Alberti was faced with a clear dictum from Vitruvius, but a different way of doing things in his own day, which even Brunelleschi had adopted. Alberti plumped for the antique precedent and in most of his buildings put it into effect. Brunelleschi had followed the precedent of Romanesque churches such as SS. Apostoli (Figure 27) and the Baptistry (Figure 51), Florence.

2   Alberti's use of antique ruins as architectural sources

Where Vitruvius gave no clear advice, or where the advice was inappropriate to fifteenth-century circumstances, Alberti was forced to turn to the ruins of antiquity which he could see everywhere around him in Rome. Alberti spent most of his life in Rome and his intense researches into everything antique had built up in him a powerfully emotional attitude towards antiquity. He was moved by the loss of so great a civilization and mourned the obscurity which surrounded so many of the ruins, the function and original form of which he could only guess at. He makes it clear in his writings that he spent a great deal of time sketching and measuring the Roman ruins.

101 The trouble was that the needs of society had changed since the Roman Empire. The biggest problem for Alberti was to find an appropriate form for the Christian church. The antique *templum* form was pagan and could not be used for a wide variety of reasons. And yet it was crucial to Alberti's hierarchy of building forms that the most important buildings in society, churches, should have the most dignified, elaborate and classical form conceivable. Vitruvius was little help: his main treatment of temples, in Book III, dealt with the conventional Roman temples, based on the Greek (Figure 66). In Chapters VII and VIII, however, he turned to 'special' temple forms. Chapter VII dealt with the Etruscan temple, to which we will return, while Chapter VIII introduced various forms of circular temple plans. These are the two chapters which interested Alberti. The circular temples reminded him of all the cosmographical and geometrical associations of the circle which Wittkower picks out (*Wittkower*, pp. 3–10). For largely theoretical reasons, he wanted to make something of the circular church plan. But the Etruscan Temple came even closer to his heart and was more practical.

102 Alberti rightly believed that the Etruscan civilization, the product of his own people, the Tuscans, had produced a culture which preceded, and rivalled in some ways, that of Rome. So when Vitruvius described an Etruscan Temple, Alberti was bound to be interested. But the description, in practice, left much to be desired (Figure 67). It should have been clear to Alberti that the temple Vitruvius was describing was small in scale, and was based on the humblest of all of the orders, the Tuscan, which was a simplified version of the Doric. The Tuscan order has very wide intercolumniations, wooden entablatures, squat columns and a generally primitive appearance. Other features of Vitruvius's description which would have disturbed Alberti were the very deep portico (half the depth of the whole building) the impractical (for church purposes) internal arrangements, with three separate parallel rooms, and the excessive diminution of the columns (they were thinner at the top by a quarter of the base diameter, giving a very stumpy look). Despite all these peculiarities, Alberti based his description of the Etruscan Temple (in Book VII) on the one described by Vitruvius, in that the overall proportions were the same (length : width is 6 : 5, in both cases). But if you examine the reconstruction of Alberti's scheme (Figure 68), you will see several differences. Read Alberti's description in *Holt* (p. 234) (beginning on the eighth line).

Figure 66

EXERCISE

List the differences briefly in your notebook.
Why do you think Alberti changed Vitruvius's description?

DISCUSSION

What Alberti has done is to take the three parallel rooms in Vitruvius's description, double them up and place them opposite each other along the sides of the building. He has placed an apse at the end of the interior and another apse in the middle of each side. He has made the portico more shallow, which means that, with the two rows of columns to fit into this depth (following Vitruvius), he had to space the columns more closely together, and thus increase the number from four in a row, to six. The order we can assume to be Ionic or Corinthian, rather than Doric (and certainly not Tuscan), because of the more narrow intercolumniation.

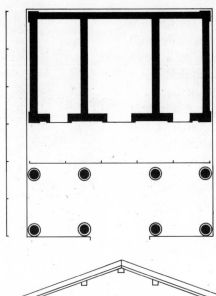

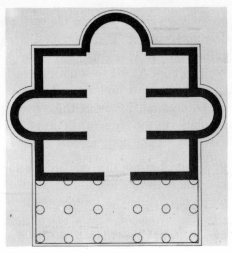

Figure 68

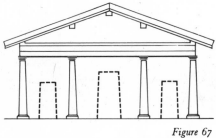

Figure 67

03 The effect of the transformation was to provide his building with a nave and side chapels, both necessary for a Christian church. He has also arrived at a plan which could be built on a larger and grander scale, with a more prestigious order and more columns in it. With these factors in mind, Alberti created a plan more suited for a great Christian church. This plan of the Etruscan Temple is the nearest thing to a practical ideal church plan in *De Re Aedificatoria*. It was later to form the basis of the plan of S. Andrea, Mantua (Figure 69). It is therefore of extreme importance, particularly since it is an 'improvement' on the original in Vitruvius. Where did Alberti get the idea for this plan?

04 The answer is exciting and revealing, for this is a case where Alberti turned to antique ruins to supply a form, where Vitruvius was of little help. One of the biggest and grandest of the ruins of antique buildings in Rome is that of the Basilica of Maxentius, completed in A.D. 313, thought to be a temple in Alberti's day (he called it the Templum Latonae) (Figure 70). Reconstructions of it in the sixteenth century usually placed two apses opposite each other in the flanks of the building, where only one had existed (Figure 71). Perhaps Alberti also thought an extra apse had existed. Now this had been a huge building, the nave being eighty feet across and over a hundred feet high, and when Alberti saw it he must have thought that this was the kind of building Vitruvius had been trying to describe as the Etruscan Temple. Although Alberti thought this had served as a temple under the Roman Empire, it had fewer of the pagan associations that normal columned temples had for people in the Renaissance. The plan bowed to none in scale and grandeur, it was more convenient for liturgical purposes than the circular plans he had toyed with, it appeared to have a pedigree not only from Vitruvius but also from antiquity itself. Writing to Lodovico Gonzaga (*c.* 1470) about the Church he was building for him in Mantua (S. Andrea), Alberti described a plan he had sent him: 'This form of temple the ancients called Sacred Etruscan. If you like it I will do a correct version in proportion.' S. Andrea in fact contains many of the features of Alberti's description of the Etruscan Temple in its internal layout (Figure 69 and cf. *Wittkower*, Plates

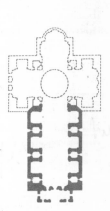

Figure 69

19a–c). The chapels are massive niches set into the wall and there are three of them on each side before the crossing. The choir and transept were only built later, and it is likely that Alberti's original intention was to place a large apse in the centre of the east end. At the west end, there is a vestibule similar to that of the Basilica of Maxentius and the massive barrel vault over the nave is also worthy of the original. Many of these features became standard in later churches, particularly in the sixteenth century, and the grandeur and Roman gravity of the whole set the tone for the High Renaissance.

105   This is the most extraordinary, but not the only adaptation Alberti made from the ruins of antiquity. Where Brunelleschi had studied the ruins without coming away with any precise models to imitate, Alberti's study of antiquity led him to incorporate the forms of several identifiable antique building types in his architecture. We will come back to this in the next section.

3   Alberti's practical advice to builders

106   I have already outlined the structure of *De Re Aedificatoria* (cf. p. 60). The first half of the treatise is about construction and utility. It is worth reading Alberti's Preface (*Holt*, pp. 218–23). Notice in particular the definition of an architect on page 219, beginning with the words: 'But before I proceed further . . . '.

107   Alberti considered that the origins of architecture were purely functional and that only at a later stage was beauty introduced as a legitimate aim, to satisfy the soul and show respect for those principles of nature which the sophisticated man learns to discern all around him. Thus, not only do the first five Books deal with the practical aspect of building, the later books, on beauty, always relate the aesthetic to the socially desirable and the functional. Alberti frowned on any architect whose aim was beauty at the expense of utility or structure.

108   Some of Alberti's advice to builders seems oddly whimsical and countrified to us. Discussing the layout of stables:

> The bone which covers the horses brain is so thin that it will bear neither damp nor cold; and therefore take care also that the moon's beams do not come in at the window; which are very apt to make him wall-eyed and to give him grievous coughs. . . .
> *De Re Aedificatoria*, Book V, Ch. XV, trans.
> Leoni.

Alberti had advice to give on everything from siting a villa to the layout of rooms, placing of windows, selection of materials, planning of towns and cities, either for a just government or for a tyranny. The text is heavily larded with classical anecdotes drawn from his learning; in this respect he imitates Vitruvius, who always had a story to hand to illustrate his dicta. But Alberti handled his classical sayings with caution. Read *Holt* (pp. 226–7) on prisons, where he introduced his remarkably humanitarian opinion in contrast to that of the ancients.

109   It becomes quite clear, when reading the first five Books, that Alberti would never sacrifice what he considered to be good contemporary practice to a rational ideal. At first, in his section on town planning in *De Re Aedificatoria*, he recommended the use of curving, elusively tortuous streets, instead of the rectangular, star-shaped or circular formations suggested by his contemporaries. In defending his choice of curving streets, Alberti puts forward tactical military grounds, but also aesthetic reasons, which makes it clear that he

was sensitive to the picturesque and human qualities of medieval townscape. Later, when describing larger cities, he turned to the wide, straight-street grid with standardized house fronts which was to be an important theme for High Renaissance planning.

10 This distinction between the grand, formal scheme of the city and the more intimate, human form of the town is typical of Alberti's attitude towards architecture. A city, he says, is like a house and a house reflects the person who lives in it, with his social position and dignity expressed in the stylistic elaboration of the building. Just as a house should not be considered except in the context of the individual environments of the town, so must the town be created out of a blending and harmonizing of the individual houses. For the humbler forms of architecture, whether on the domestic or civic scale, Alberti gives the patron and builder a very free hand. Their aim should be simple, to build soundly and conveniently and not waste money on unnecessary pretention.

> Moreover, in relating the parts [of a house] to each other, follow the example of nature's simplicity. As in everything else, we must praise sobriety, just as we must reprove an excessive zeal for building. The parts must be moderately scaled and relating precisely to the functions they are to serve. For if we think about it, all architecture was born out of necessity, was reared by convenience, and matured through usage. Only then was pleasure taken into consideration but this pleasure will be spoilt by any kind of excess. Thus we must plan a building in such a way that nothing which is necessary be left out and that nothing that is retained could be criticized from any point of view.
>
> *De Re Aedificatoria*, Book I, Ch. IX, Orlandi, pp. 66–7, trans. T.B.

11 Here we have a completely practical, common-sense definition of the criteria of building, which can be read either as a historical development or as a cumulative process in designing. The practical considerations must be considered first and perfected; any defects in these will spoil any formal beauty which the building may have.

4   Alberti's theory of architectural proportions

12 To understand why Alberti arrived at his proportional theory, we must begin with the theory of beauty which arose directly from his practical advice to builders.

EXERCISE

Read *Holt* (pp. 229–31). Compare this passage with the one cited above (paragraph 110).

1   Has Alberti contradicted himself?

2   Pick out Alberti's definitions of beauty.

3   How would Alberti set about answering the question 'Is this building beautiful'?

DISCUSSION

1   At first sight, Alberti appears to have discarded the emphasis on necessity and convenience. But you must remember that this passage comes at the beginning of the four Books on *venustas*, beauty. He is slightly exaggerating his points to make them effective. He still insists that a building should be, '*not only* useful and convenient, *but also* handsomely adorned'. So the search for beauty is an attribute of a sophisticated culture, where the soul must be satisfied, as well as the body.

2   The two definitions of beauty begin on line 32, p. 230 and line 9, p. 231, *Holt*.

3   Alberti would answer by first asking the questions, 'Could anything be added to this to make it more perfect?' and, 'Could anything be taken away from this, or altered, without marring it?'

He would in fact be relying on his intuitive judgement and common sense, much as he did when discussing house plans in Book I (see above, paragraph 110).

113   Alberti's aim in all his judgements, is to arrive at an Aristotelian mean, the happy mean between two extremes (e.g. not too hot, not too cold, but just right). Alberti believed that the key to beauty lay in discovering the 'Laws of Nature', which he considered to be universally valid.

> Whoever wishes to be praised, as any sane man must, for the buildings he undertakes, must rely on precise and unchanging rules; creating with rules of this kind is central to (all) art.
>
> *De Re Aedificatoria*, Book VI, Ch. II, Orlandi, pp. 448–9, trans. T.B.

[cf. *Holt*, p. 231, line 15. Leoni's assumption that Alberti meant *proportion* when he wrote 'precise and unchanging rules' ('hos certa sane moveri ratione') is not a bad guess.]

But there was a difference between those 'precise and unchanging rules' which could be concretely defined, and those which were in some way beyond definitions. Alberti tackled this problem by selecting certain areas where he felt his knowledge would give him concrete answers. Read *Holt*, pp. 234–8.

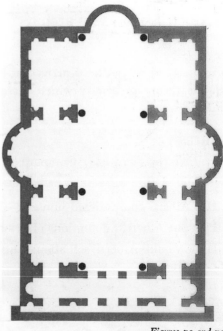

Figures 70 and 71

4   On page 236 Leoni translated the latin words *numerus*, *finitio* and *collocatio* rather literally as *Number*, *Finishing* and *Collocation*. These Latin words, apart from *numerus*, are really untranslatable, since Alberti used them in a special way. *Finitio* was defined by Alberti as follows:

> We take *finitio* to refer to the mutual relationships between the lines [in a building or architectural plan] which are defined by the dimensions [*numerus*]. Such lines are: length, breadth, height.
>
> *De Re Aedificatoria*, Book IX, Ch. V, Orlandi, pp. 820–1, trans. T.B.

For Alberti, *finitio* means something quite close to 'proportion'. Wittkower translated it as 'harmonic relations' (*Wittkower*, p. 110). *Collocatio* refers to the effective placing and arrangement of parts:

> Finally, *collocatio*. This has to do with the situation and positioning of the parts. One finds it easier to point out when it has failed than define the right way of acquiring it. In fact it depends to a great extent on an innate faculty of judgement in the human soul, and yet it shares many of the principles on which *finitio* is based.
>
> *De Re Aedificatoria*, Book IX, Ch. VII, Orlandi, p. 836, trans. T.B.

5   Further down on page 236, Leoni translated the very important word *concinnitas* as *Congruity*. This concept refers to that final, all-embracing harmony and blending together which gathers together all the formal relationships of the building and unites them in a beautiful effect. *Concinnitas* tells us little about beauty, since it is practically synonymous with it in Alberti's mind.

> The aim and purpose of *concinnitas* is to take parts [of a building], which are normally quite different from each other, and, by applying precise rules, coordinate them in such a way that they can be seen to fit together perfectly.
>
> *De Re Aedificatoria*, Book IX, Ch. V, Orlandi, pp. 814–5, trans. T.B.

In the original, the definition is rather less circular than in Leoni's translation (cf. *Holt*, p. 236, line 32) where beauty is made an attribute of *concinnitas*. Even in the original, Alberti gives us little help in deciding how to tell whether parts 'fit together perfectly'. In the last resort, Alberti would ask himself whether the effect 'looked right'. But with *finitio* and *numerus*, he felt he was on safer ground, where certain rules had been laid down, since these two qualities were subject to the 'scientific' disciplines of arithmetic, geometry, cosmography and musical theory.

EXERCISE

I would like you to look again at what Wittkower has to say about Alberti's proportional theory, in particular pages 33, 101–26. Much of this concerns other writers and architects, but applying the general picture to Alberti's thought, and remembering that, in *De Re Aedificatoria*, proportional theory is considered almost entirely under the heading of *finitio*, try to give your own answer now to the second question set in Part III of this unit (paragraph 88).

DISCUSSION

1   Alberti was no mere builder, he was a scholar in his own right interested in discovering the laws of nature which governed proportions as part of learning how to build well.

2   When presented with relationships between numbers, his mind immediately took in the range of associations Wittkower has outlined. He would think of Plato's mathematical analogy for the universe (*Wittkower*, p. 104), Pythagorean mathematical proportions derived from music (*Wittkower*, pp. 33 and 103), the mean proportionals attributed to Pythogoras but expounded in Porphyry's *Commentary on Ptolemy's Harmonics* (*Wittkower*, p. 109, note 4 and pp. 110–12). He would also think of Vitruvius's claim that the human form represented divine proportions, fitting into a circle and a square (*Wittkower*, p. 101), and this would confirm for him the idea that, at all levels, certain laws of nature were reflected in the universe which could be explained in mathematical terms.

3   Having said all that, we must recognize that Alberti reserved many aspects of his analysis of beauty in architecture for a less precise, more personal judgement. He laid stress on mathematical solutions primarily because of the weight of evidence available to him. But he never attempted to apply these theories to all buildings or to every use of numbers and spaces.

116   Alberti's explanation of how architects should decide on which numbers to use (his exposition of *numerus* in Book IX, Chapter V), turns out to be nothing more than the listing of the associations that all the numbers from *3–10* had for him. These associations were partly mathematical, partly astrological, partly religious and partly conventional (handing on generally agreed properties of numbers). He made no attempt to select useful numbers for the architect's use. In particular, he did not indicate that some numbers, such as *5* and *7*, would not fit easily into his theory of proportions. There are very few examples of Alberti's use of his proportional theories in the text of *De Re Aedificatoria*. Most surprisingly, his pet project, the plan of the Etruscan Temple (Figure 68), contains very few proportional relationships. Where he does make use of part of his theory, he indicates to us that a slavish use of proportions based on the body or on other analogies can itself be suspect. In Chapter VII, Book IX, he explains how he thought the ancients arrived at the proportions of their columns. First they noted that a man's width went into his height six times, but that the distance between his umbilical cord and his groin went into it ten times. Alberti immediately remembers approvingly that *1 : 6* and *1: 10* were the proportions of Noah's ark. He then points out that, 'through that spontaneous sensibility, born of the spirit, which is aroused by . . . *concinnitas*', the ancients renounced both these extremes and arrived at the arithmetical mean of *6* and *10*, to give *8* (1 : 8 is the Ionic proportion) the mean of *6* and *8*, to give *7* (1 : 7 is the Doric proportion) and *8* and *10* to give *9* (1 : 9 is the Corinthian proportion). This use of his theories shows how pragmatic Alberti's attitudes were; he always insisted on the final arbitration of the 'spontaneous sensibility' born of the spirit: to modify the 'divine' proportions of Nature.

117   Read *Holt*, pp. 238–43 (notice especially Alberti's first-hand account of the process of creation, p. 242, lines 19–30). The significance of all this rests on Alberti's reliance on 'spontaneous sensibility'. In his art theory, he never claimed that there was any alternative to man's own reasoned judgements in deciding whether something was beautiful. Each case must be judged on its own merits, and the architect should not expect any one rational principle to supply all the answers. So when we come to Alberti's buildings, we must not expect a totally comprehensive and consistent use of harmonic proportional theory.

PART V ALBERTI'S ARCHITECTURE

A code 0313 5 5073   FFF, Ro, Ri FM FFA

18 We have already seen that Alberti's architectural career was a late development in his life. Although the first documented involvement in a full-scale architectural commission dates from 1450, we must assume that he had been gathering information and expertise in architectural matters since 1429, when he was already in contact with Brunelleschi. Even in his non-artistic writings, such as *Della Famiglia* (1433/4), he liked to use architectural anecdotes to illustrate his arguments. And from 1447, at Pope Nicholas V's accession, it seems certain that Alberti was already involved in advising on the large scale architectural schemes undertaken in Rome.

Della Famiglia

Lionello D'este

19 A summary of Alberti's architectural activities is as follows:

1443   Consulted by Lionello d'Este over a monument to Nicholas I in Ferrara. Typically, Alberti recommended for the equestrian statue a tall base in the form of a triumphal arch. He also recommended, for the campanile of the Cathedral at Ferrara, superimposed orders, a form largely followed from then on (see paragraph 137).

1447–1453   Advised Nicholas V on repairs and new constructions in Rome, including the restoration of many early Christian churches, including old St. Peters and S. Stefano Rotondo and repairing aqueducts.

1450   Given the task of rebuilding the outside of S. Francesco, Rimini (Figures 80 and 82), by Sigismondo Malatesta. In this he supervised the work of Matteo de' Pasti, who was restoring the interior.

1446–1451   Designed the façade of the Palazzo Rucellai, Florence (Figure 72), which was carried out, with variations, by Bernardo Rossellino (see page 77).

1455–1470   Alberti restored the façade of S. Maria Novella, Florence (Figure 32).

1460–1470   Alberti provided designs and instructions for S. Sebastiano, Mantua, for Ludovico Gonzaga, the first of a series of undertakings for this patron.

1460–1466   Loggia dei Rucellai. Design attributed to Alberti.

1467   The tomb of the Holy Sepulchre (Figure 59) and the Cappella Rucellai in which it stands in what was the Church of S. Pancrazio, Florence.

1470   Alberti provided the scheme for S. Andrea, Mantua (Figure 69). Both these Mantua Churches were built by Luca Fancelli.

Several other buildings are attributed to him, mostly in Rome and Florence; some of them are interesting as examples of his influence, whatever the uncertainties of authorship.

20 It is clearly impossible, in the remaining pages of this unit, to investigate Alberti's architecture in all its aspects. Scholars disagree about the timing and the nature of his involvement in the buildings discussed. My aim is to investigate the way his architectural principles, outlined in the last section, are reflected in his buildings. And I'm going to single out three themes. First, Alberti's use of the 'classical language' of architecture and his 'correctness' by the standards of his own treatise. Secondly, some examples of his proportional theory. Thirdly, the additions he made to Renaissance building vocabulary by the adaptation of certain antique building forms to new uses. In each of these sections, despite the important stress on the *classical*, you will see how Alberti has developed and altered his sources, to create completely new forms which were to dominate Renaissance architectural style in the sixteenth century.

1   Alberti's use of the 'classical language of antiquity' in his architecture

121   We have already seen what stress Alberti placed on learning from antiquity (cf. especially *Holt*, p. 240, lines 2–33). In general it can be said that Alberti set new standards of classicism in his buildings. But in many instances, his details, like those of Brunelleschi, owe more to his imagination than to exact antique sources. For instance, his use of heraldic detail, embodying the emblems and crests of his patrons, resulted in several highly effective forms. The Rucellai wind-blown sail appears not only in the frieze of the Palazzo Rucellai (Figures 72 and 73), but also in the church façade commissioned by Giovanni Rucellai (Figure 32), S. Maria Novella.

122   Some of Alberti's capitals are impressive as faithful versions of the antique originals. For instance, the Corinthian capitals on the façade of S. Maria Novella (Figure 74). But Alberti frequently made use of a much simplifed Corinthian, notably on the Palazzo Rucellai (Figure 73) and the two capitals belonging to the pilasters flanking the great central arch of the façade of S. Andrea, Mantua (which, however, was erected after Alberti's death). These freer versions have the flattened, linear, quality of many contemporary examples. The Composite capitals of the façade of S. Franceso, Rimini, are even more bizarre, but curiously classical in feeling, if not in detail.

123   Alberti's Doric capitals seem very wayward when compared to the close copies from antiquity publicized by Palladio in his *Four Books of Architecture* over a hundred years later (Figure 75). Those on the façade of S. Maria Novella and the Palazzo Rucellai are typical (Figures 74 and 76). We might be tempted

Figure 73

Figure 74

to consider these the work of the workmen in charge (Alberti rarely supervised work in progress in person), were it not for the fact that the description of the Doric capital in *De Re Aedificatoria* comes quite close to those on the Palazzo Rucellai (Figure 76). He must have preferred the stumpy proportions of these capitals to other 'correct' examples he could have seen in Rome among the ruins. Typically, he makes it clear in the description that the architect is free to vary the decoration as he sees fit, and he has taken this liberty himself, adding the fluting to the neck of the capital and a band of egg-and-dart moulding to its top.

24   Although these Doric capitals seem unclassical to us now, conditioned by the sixteenth-century theorists like Vignola and Palladio, there were sound antique precedents to be found. But Alberti's models were to be superseded in the classical canon by capitals like Palladio's (see Figure 75).

2   Alberti's practical application of his proportional theory

25   All of Alberti's church façades can be inscribed in a square, even where he had to squash them in, as at S. Andrea, where the crowning pediment is too low for correctness. In all his designs, we can immediately identify basic, simple relationships such as $1 : 1$ and $1 : 2$. But we must always remember that Brunelleschi had incorporated such relationships in a plan like that of S. Spirito with great consistency. When we realize, furthermore, that these relationships in turn were largely derived from the Romanesque church of SS. Apostoli, it is clear that a certain amount of caution must be used in identifying a complex proportional theory such as Alberti's.

126   Medieval architects had employed a variety of arithmetical and geometrical aids in planning their buildings. Usually, these aids were used for convenience in setting out the ground plan and employed units of measurement such as the yardstick, with which a builder could measure out the plan. But Wittkower's contention is that Alberti consciously used the diameter of the columns as modules with which to construct the proportions of his façades and that he used his proportional theories consistently throughout his designs to link together all the elements in a harmonic whole.

127   You may have thought, in reading Wittkower's account of the façade of S. Maria Novella (*Wittkower*, p. 46), that the ratios he finds there appear arbitrary, or perhaps accidental. Let's look at the façade again. The Gothic lower storey originally had five narrow bays on each side marked by pointed arches applied to the wall (Alberti masked the end ones with his striped pilasters and columns) and with a larger opening in the middle. The effect of Alberti's positioning of his four Corinthian columns was to divide up this lower storey so that if its width is divided into eight equal divisions (or 'units') (each one six times the column-diameter), two would fall in the central bay, and three on each side (Figure 77). This fits in well, since the height from the ground to the main entablature under the attic also measures three of these 'units', so that there are two squares (of three 'units' each side) on either side of the central bay, with a central bay with sides measuring 2×3 (or the ratio of $1 : 1\frac{1}{2}$). The whole lower storey therefore comes out at 8×3 of these 'units'. To bring it up to a $1 : 2$ rectangle, Alberti added an attic right across the façade (1 'unit' high, thus making a rectangle of 8×4 (Figure 78)). So we can now read the lower storey up to the top of the attic as two squares of 4 'units' each. A square of 4×4 'units' was then added to become the upper storey, leaving two 'empty' rectangles of 2×2 'units' (Figure 79).[1]

128   I hope you can see how these proportional ratios work. They have a practical, designing function, allowing Alberti to introduce three different sizes of 'square' (8×8, 4×4, 3×3) without having any untidy left-overs. But where does the column-diameter fit in?

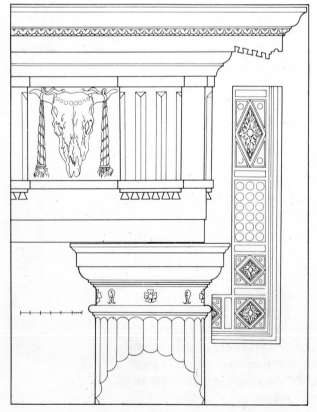

Figure 75

[1] Figures 77, 78 and 79 are on page 74.

EXERCISE

1   How many times does the column-diameter go into the width of the façade?

2   Corinthian columns are supposed to be nine times their diameter in height. Approximately how high are the columns here in terms of their diameter?

3   Why didn't Alberti make his Corinthian columns the right height for their width?

P. Rucellai ground floor.

Figure 76
(cf. note in Appendix II)

DISCUSSION

1   The column-diameters go into the attic six times (cf. *Wittkower*, p. 46). So they go into the façade width (or height) forty-eight times.

2   Approximately fourteen column-diameters high.

3   Alberti had a choice. Either he could have shortened the columns to nine diameters. They would then have extended only to one and a half of our 'squares' in Figure 79. Even with very high pedestals, he could not have made columns this high reach the entablature. If he had doubled the diameters of the columns, retaining a simple proportion between the diameters and the 'squares', the resulting columns would have been too high. They would have extended right up to the base of the attic, allowing no room for an entablature.

29   I would suggest that this is evidence that Alberti was keen to preserve the relationship between his column-diameters and the dimensions of his façade. Don't worry if this seems very complicated. The main point to take away is that Alberti seems to have sacrificed an article of classical dogma (that the height of a Corinthian column should be nine times its diameter) in his eagerness to ensure that the column-diameter should retain a fixed, commensurate ratio with the main dimensions of the façade.

130   A similar exercise could be carried out with the façade of S. Francesco, Rimini, where the columns are a third of the façade in height and where the main square of the façade is divided into six rectangles in the proportion of 2 : 3 by the central pair of columns (Figure 80).

131   The answer to part (a) of Question 3 in Part III (paragraph 88) then, is that there certainly is evidence that Alberti put his proportional theories into effect in some buildings, but we must be careful not to attribute to him more consistency and dogmatism than the claimed for himself in *De Re Aedificatoria*. There are inconsistencies in the proportions of all his buildings and we must assume that these result as much from his modification of the rules to meet other requirements as from his own or his workmen's inability to put the rules into effect.

Figures 77, 78 and 79

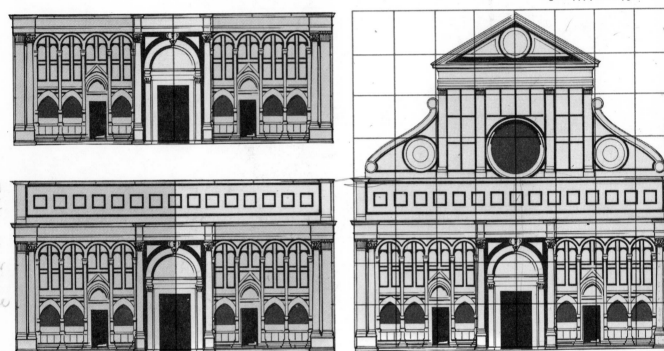

3   Alberti's adaptation of antique building forms to new uses

132   Probably the greatest single difference between Alberti and Brunelleschi in their attitude towards the antique is that Alberti was constantly on the look-out for antique buildings which he could adapt to modern uses. We have already seen how he made use of the Basilica of Maxentius to help him out in reconstructing Vitruvius's Etruscan Temple (paragraph 104).

133   In a letter to Matteo de' Pasti (who was working on the interior of S. Francesco, Rimini) dated 18 November 1454, Alberti wrote:

> But as for what you tell me Manetto [not the Manetti who wrote the Life of Brunelleschi] says about cupolas having to be twice as high as they are wide, I for my part have more faith in those who built the Terme [Roman Baths] and the Pantheon and all those noble edifices, than in him, and a great deal more in reason than in any man.
>
> D. S. Chambers (1970) (ed.) *Patrons and Artists in the Italian Renaissance*, Macmillan, p. 182.

The Pantheon is a great circular domed temple (dating originally from the early Roman Empire but completely rebuilt in its present form in the second century A.D.), whose internal height is equal to its diameter (Figure 81). The letter quoted above has led many scholars to suppose that the dome Alberti intended to build over the east end of S. Francesco, would not have been raised on a drum, as appears in Matteo de' Pasti's medal (Figure 82), but would have been derived from a circle drawn from the mid point of the façade (Figure 80). Here, then is circumstantial evidence at least that Alberti would have adopted a highly prestigious form of antique dome in preference to the kind of high, pointed dome (rising from a high octagonal drum) created by the Opera del Duomo and Brunelleschi for the Cathedral in Florence.

134 Another circular plan with which Alberti became involved is described by Wittkower (*Wittkower*, p. 6) (Figure 83). The choir of SS. Annunziata had been begun by Michelozzo on a circular plan, was continued and adapted slightly by Antonio Manetti and Alberti. It was Alberti's patron Ludovico Gonzaga who put up the money to finish the church, and Alberti had to defend the circular form for the choir against the charge that a circular plan was suitable for mausolea only. The plan is based on that of S. Maria degli Angeli (Figure 45).

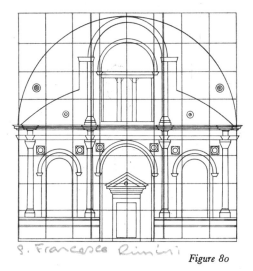

S. Francesco Rimini

Figure 80

Matteo de Pasti's model of A' design for S. Francesco Ri

Figure 82

PANTHEON. Rome, Cross Section

Figure 81

135   Alberti adapted the Roman Triumphal Arch in a most important way, which is indicative of a more revolutionary approach to antique forms. Wittkower explains how Alberti based the façade of S. Francesco on the triumphal arch (*Wittkower*, pp. 37–41). The whole façade can be interpreted as a symbolic reference to the triumph over death, so that the symbolic association with Roman triumphal arches may have been deliberate. If you look carefully at the façade (Figure 80), you will see that its breadth is divided into eight approximately equal units, the solid parts alternating equally with the hollow, except for the middle bay, which is twice the width of the others. Now this is precisely the way Alberti articulated the triumphal arch he described in *De Re Aedificatoria* (Figure 84). Another feature in S. Franceso which recalls Roman triumphal arches is the treatment of the columns and the entablature. The entablature is 'broken' forward over the columns, so that a vertical rhythm is maintained. Wittkower also analyses Alberti's development of the triumphal arch motif in the façade of S. Andrea, Mantua (*Wittkower*, pp. 53–5).

136   When Filarete (cf. *Holt*, p. 243) wanted to cite an example of a building constructed according to 'il modo antico' (the antique manner), he cited the Palazzo Rucellai in Florence. You can read the passage in *Holt* (pp. 247–8). The Palazzo Rucellai in the via della Vigna, Florence (Figure 72), is mentioned in the top line of page 248. What was it about this Palace that he considered to exemplify the antique style?

137   In Book XIII, Chapter VII, of *De Re Aedificatoria*, Alberti refers to 'rows of colonnades one over another, in imitation of houses . . . '. No examples of antique houses with superimposed orders of columns or pilasters were known in Alberti's day, but from this remark it seems clear that Alberti thought they would have had such an arrangement. What makes this interesting is that the passage belongs to an account of Roman theatres, where such super-imposed orders could still be seen (Figure 85). Examples which remain to this day are the Theatre of Marcellus and the Colloseum.

138   What made the Palazzo Rucellai 'antique', then, was Alberti's adaptation of the superimposed orders of Roman theatres and amphitheatres to domestic architecture, perhaps in the belief that Roman houses also had had this arrangement. You can see the three orders of pilasters, Doric, Corinthian and Corinthian on the Palazzo Rucellai (Figure 72). To be completely 'correct' the superimposed orders should have had the regular progression of Doric, *Ionic* and Corinthian, and should have diminished by a fixed proportion of their height on each successive storey. But after the courtyard of the Palazzo Venezia[1] had been built in Rome in the 1460s, influenced by Alberti, the fashion for superimposed orders of pilasters or half-columns attached to wall arches came to dominate domestic architecture. Here again, Alberti found in antiquity a form which he could adapt for modern requirements and set a standard for later periods.

EXERCISE

How would you answer part (b) of Question 3 in paragraph 88?

DISCUSSION

1   We have considerable evidence that Alberti made use of his study of antiquity, adapting many classical forms for new uses.

2   He allowed himself considerable freedom in his use of these antique forms.

1 See Figure 86.

His use of them was partly to do with the solution of planning and designing problems (such as how to design a church façade when there were no precedents in antiquity).

3   Occasionally, Alberti used the associations with the antique form he was borrowing to enrich the symbolic quality of a building. Such is the case with his adaptations from the triumphal arch.

Figure 72

77

PART VI   CONCLUSIONS ON ARCHITECTURAL THEORY AND THE FLORENTINE RENAISSANCE

139   Classicism and modernity, these were the themes we began with. Alberti and Brunelleschi were both committed to a style which would be on the one hand more *classical* (that is, more like the architecture of the ancients), but also more *modern* (which could be paraphrased as scientific, philosophical or knowledgeable). Phrased like this, we can place on the classical side of our distinction all those influences which caused Brunelleschi and Alberti to do away with 'incorrect' architectural solutions, getting rid of the gothic pier, the pointed arch, superfluous ornament and so on. Also all those influences which, interpreted and changed in the minds of the architects, were transformed into a new context, such as the triumphal arch form, the superimposed orders of Alberti's Palazzo Rucellai and the metamorphosis of the Basilica of Maxentius into a Christian church at S. Andrea.

140   On the other side of the distinction, we must count Alberti's and Brunelleschi's experiments with perspective, with proportional theory, with a 'look' which is neither antique nor Tuscan Romanesque, but a subtle mixture of both.

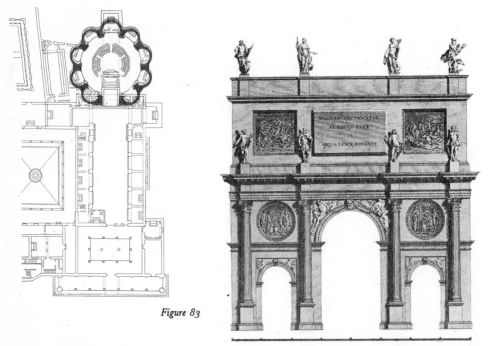

Figure 83

Figure 84

Incidentally, we must be very careful in our use of the word 'modern'. In the Renaissance, this meant 'Gothic' and, therefore, 'barbaric' or 'bad'. By 'modern' I only wish to indicate the attitude of progressive innovation shared by both architects. Despite the continuity, which is never broken, between the Middle Ages and the Renaissance, we still have to recognize that the style of the Renaissance in the fifteenth century was an innovation, as sudden as any development in the history of architecture. The coherence behind the stylistic changes which define the Renaissance was provided by the efforts of men like Brunelleschi and Alberti who provided a framework of ideas, a rationale for the new architecture, which could combine the antique and the modern. Alberti made it absolutely clear that the architect should not merely copy antiquity, he should be always on the lookout for ways of improving on his sources.

41   I hope you will recapitulate this unit by looking back over all the illustrations and asking yourself these questions:

1   Could Brunelleschi's and Alberti's architecture have developed as it did without the new interest in the architecture of antiquity?

2   In what ways was Alberti's interest in the architecture of antiquity more important in the formation of his buildings than it was for Brunelleschi?

3   What, if any, was the connection in the minds of these two architects between their interest in proportional and perspectival theory, and their interest in antiquity?

DISCUSSION

1   It seems clear to me that it could not.
(a)   There are so many classical details, such as the orders and all their constituent parts, a reliance on the round arch, the dome, and countless other particulars taken from antiquity. To 'see' this point clearly, you only have to go back to the comparison between the Cathedral and S. Lorenzo.
(b)   On the other hand, we must not underestimate the importance of native Tuscan models such as the Baptistry, churches like SS. Apostoli, S. Miniato al Monte, etc.

2   The key difference seems to me to lie in the use Alberti made of whole antique building types, whereas Brunelleschi adapted Romanesque and Gothic forms to the classical idiom.

3   (a)   They both felt that the authors of antiquity, from Plato onwards, held the key to these fields of knowledge, if this key could only be discovered.
(b)   Both associated all forms of knowledge and discovery with the acquisition of the learning of antiquity. At times, they were perhaps over respectful. As much as anything, this is an accident due to the humanist circles to which they belonged, which shared this confusion between the new and the antique. This was a period when so many exciting discoveries were being made about antiquity that it was assumed that the ancients knew everything that needed knowing. At the same time, the Ancients did not know everything; Alberti knew that they had not mastered perspective and always placed his final trust in his own reason. So here at least Brunelleschi and Alberti went beyond Antiquity consciously. And Brunelleschi in particular was well aware of his own inventiveness and originality. His contemporaries were prepared on occasion to say that he had improved on the ancients, and presumably he shared this view.

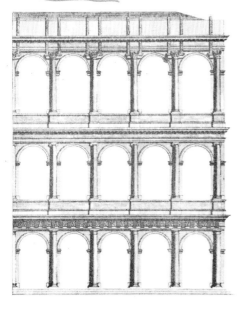

Figures 85 and 86

APPENDIX II

Notes to the Figures

25 *The nave of Chartres Cathedral*. This, the first of the great High Gothic Cathedrals of France, epitomizes the Northern Gothic style at its grandest. The effect of height and complexity of surface are accentuated by the composite piers and the maximum penetration and moulding of the walls. The Cathedral was begun in 1194.

26 *S. Maria del Fiore*. For the early history of Florence Cathedral, see Unit 7. The nave was vaulted in 1378, the aisles in 1380. The crossing was completed up to the drum of the dome in the next forty years. The simplicity of the decoration disguises its scale; the nave and aisles measure nearly 150 feet across.

27 *SS. Apostoli*. Late eleventh century. The side chapels retain their fifteenth-century decoration but the nave has been restored to its original form. The Composite capitals are copies of antique spoils from the Roman Baths.

28 *S. Lorenzo*. Built by Antonio Manetti between 1447–60 according to Brunelleschi's plans (1420). The order is Corinthian and its members are in dark *pietra serena*, contrasting with white wall surfaces. The blocks above the capitals correspond exactly with the architrave, frieze and cornice of the normal entablature (cf. glossary, p. 46 and Figure 64).

29 *Loggia dei Lanzi*. Perhaps designed by Jacopo Orcagna (active 1369–98), built 1376–82, by Benci di Cione and Simone di Francesco Talenti. It stands to the right of the Palazzo Vecchio and was used for public ceremonies.

30 *S. Miniato al Monte*. Rebuilt from 1018, it was only finished at the beginning of the thirteenth century. The white and green marble decoration owes something to the Baptistry (cf. Figure 51).

31 *Loggia degli Innocenti*. By Fillipo Brunelleschi, 1419–26. This loggia runs along the façade of the Foundling Hospital, founded in 1419 by the Arte della Seta. The circular 'tondi' with the *terracotta* swaddled babies, are by Andrea della Robbia, from the 1480s.

32 *S. Maria Novella*. The present church was begun in 1246. The façade around 1300. The façade was left unfinished and completed by Alberti (at the expense of the Rucellai family), the date inscribed in the entablature under the pediment. For further details see p. 72.

33 *Loggia dei Lanzi, capital*. See Figure 29.

34 *S. Maria Novella, capital*. One of the left aisle capitals, dating from the thirteenth century. See Figure 32.

35 *S. Lorenzo, capital*. See Figure 28.

36 *Baptistry, capital*. Originally the church of S. Giovanni, it was used for a time as the Cathedral of Florence (1059–1128). The exterior dates from between the eleventh and twelfth centuries. Many antique spoils were included among the details. This capital is a good copy from the antique (see Figure 56).

38   *Cross-section of the Cupola of Florence Cathedral*, showing the twin shell construction (for a view up between the shells, cf. Figure 52). Compare the relatively steep, light section with the hemispherical, heavy dome of the Pantheon (cf. Figure 81).

39   *View of the crossing, San Lorenzo* (see below, Figure 43).

40   *S. Lorenzo, nave bay* (see below, Figure 44).

41   *Interior of the Old Sacristy, S. Lorenzo* (1421–29). It has the double function of sacristy and burial chapel for the man who paid for it, Giovanni de' Medici, who is buried right under the dome. The relief decoration and the little doorways left and right of the altar are by Donatello (later 1430s); they are completely un-Brunelleschian in style, and Brunelleschi wrote sonnets disclaiming responsibility for them.

42   *Interior of the Pazzi Chapel* (designed *c.* 1429). The chapel has the double function of chapter house and Pazzi family chapel. The scheme is a combination of the traditional scheme for chapter houses (a rectangle with a square altar chapel attached) and the two dome arrangement of the Old Sacristy. Unlike the Old Sacristy the pilaster articulation is carried round all four walls.

43   *View of the crossing, S. Spirito* (compare with Figure 39). At S. Lorenzo, Brunelleschi had to build on the transept foundation which had been begun in 1419, two years before he took over as architect in 1421. This prevented him from producing a unified solution for the nave (with columns) and transepts (without). The last bay of the side walls of the nave is closed, as it is the side wall of one of the transept chapels (cf. the Plan, Figure 49). At S. Spirito (Figure 43), where he was completely free, he produced a unified system, and a harmonious transition from nave to transept, by carrying the nave colonnade right round the church. The columns are answered by half columns on the aisle walls, dividing the chapels, which are blended into the main space by very rich, curving mouldings (cf. the Plan of S. Spirito, Figure 46).

44   *S. Spirito, nave bay* (designed 1434–36) (compare with Figure 40). This comparison exemplifies the main differences between Brunelleschi's two great churches, as well as the differences between his later and earlier architecture. Bases, capitals, entablature blocks, and the contrast of grey on white are the same. But in S. Lorenzo there are rectangular side chapels, with pilasters between them; in S. Spirito these flat forms are replaced by the curving forms of half columns and semi-circular chapels. In S. Lorenzo the chapels are low recesses off the central space of the church; in Santo Spirito the chapels are the same height as the nave arcades, and become part of a single unified space. In San Lorenzo the mouldings are crisp and hard, emphasizing the spatial distinctness of each chapel, while in Santo Spirito they are rounded, leading the eye smoothly from chapel to chapel. It is worth noting that Manetti records Brunelleschi as saying that in S. Spirito he had begun a church 'after his own intention', implying a certain dissatisfaction with S. Lorenzo.

45   *Plan of S. Maria degli Angeli*. Brunelleschi's most completely centralized church project. It was never finished but had a profound influence on later architects.

46   *Plan of S. Spirito*. Brunelleschi intended the semi-circular chapels to appear on the outside (as in the black part of the plan). They are now hidden behind a straight wall (shaded). He also planned four doors for the façade

and a continuation of the columns round the inside of the west end. These intended parts are indicated in the insert below.

47   *Exedra at the base of the Cupola, Florence Cathedral.* One of the four identical exedrae, based on a design by Brunelleschi approved in 1439. Though relatively small, their deep niches and paired half columns play an essential part in the monumental build up towards the cupola itself. They make a perfect visual transition from the lower part of the cathedral to the dome itself, and in them Brunelleschi created a new type of exterior monumental architecture.

48   Plan of S. Trinità (later fourteenth century). This is very close to the plan of S. Lorenzo (cf. Figure 49).

49   Plan of S. Lorenzo. Brunelleschi probably intended to have square nave chapels. The more shallow, rectangular ones were built for reasons of economy.

50   Donatello, *The Raising of Drusiana*, Old Sacristy (between 1437 and 1443). One of the four painted *terracotta* reliefs in the pendentives by Donatello, with stories of St. John the Evangelist (patron saint of Giovanni de' Medici) to whom the chapel is dedicated. The architecture is completely un-Brunelleschian. With its massive barrel vault, and supporting piers, it recalls ancient Roman structures, and anticipates Alberti. For another example, cf. Figure 23, in which Doric capitals with decorations very similar to those on Alberti's Palazzo Rucellai can be seen (cf. Figure 74).

51   *View of the Baptistry from the central door of the cathedral.* This photograph (1971) is taken from the same position from which Brunelleschi painted the Baptistry in order to display the effectiveness of his new perspective system. The photograph shows a little less, at top and bottom, than Brunelleschi's panel, which is described in detail by Manetti (see *Holt*, pp. 170–3).

52   *View of the space between the two shells of the Cupola, Florence Cathedral.* Despite their very different external appearance, structurally the Baptistry dome was Brunelleschi's chief model for the cupola. Like the cupola it has an inner and outer shell (cf. Figure 38), and in addition to the corner ribs, the two shells are joined by two concealed ribs on each of the eight sides.

53   *View of the space between the two shells of the Baptistry dome.*

54   *Capital, Old Sacristy* (designed *c.* 1421).

55   Giotto, painted capital, *Ascension of the Evangelist*, Peruzzi Chapel, S. Croce (probably before 1335). The capital type which Brunelleschi designed for the Old Sacristy was used by him in all his later works. Although it is recognizably Corinthian, he must deliberately have made it different from ancient Roman examples (cf. Figure 56) or good copies (cf. Figure 36). The leaves are less naturalistic, the volutes do not grow out of the foliage below, the inner volutes are equal in size to the outer ones. This simplification is in line with the simplifying and rationalizing tendencies of Brunelleschi's style. A likely source is Giotto's capital, which would also have been symbolically appropriate, as it appears on the building from which St. John the Evangelist (to whom the Old Sacristy is dedicated) ascended into heaven.

56   *Corinthian capital* from the interior of the Pantheon, drawn by Palladio, from *The Four Books of Architecture* (Dover, 1965). A very finely worked example of the antique type (cf. Figure 36).

57 *The plan of the Old Sacristy, S. Lorenzo*, consists of two domed squares (cf. Figure 61). The niches in the altar chapel, which are segments of a single circle, may well have been introduced in imitation of the Holy Sepulchre at Jerusalem (cf. Figure 58).

58 *The plan of the Palace chapel at Castiglione d'Olona*, north of Milan (*c.* 1440). The style of the chapel is Brunelleschian. The dedication is to the body of Christ. In keeping with this, the chapel was built in imitation of the Holy Sepulchre in Jerusalem.

59 *The lantern of the 'Holy Sepulchre' in the Rucellai chapel, S. Pancrazio.* Designed by Alberti, on the basis of measurements made in Jerusalem and built in the early 1460s.

60 *Top of the Old Sacristy Lantern (1428 inscribed on it).* This is the original spirally fluted top, removed from the building and replaced by a replica during restoration. The unusual form was almost certainly inspired by the lantern on top of the Holy Sepulchre in Jerusalem, and significantly this feature is repeated on top of Alberti's replica of the Holy Sepulchre in the Rucellai Chapel in S. Pancrazio (see Figure 59). See also the note to Figure 62.

61 *The Baptistry of Padua Cathedral* (thirteenth century) is so close in plan, elevation and measurements to the Old Sacristy that Brunelleschi must have had it in mind when he made his design (cf. Figures 41 and 57).

62 Taddeo Gaddi, *Presentation of the Virgin*, Baroncelli Chapel, S. Croce, *c.* 1332–37.
This imaginary reconstruction of the Temple at Jerusalem differs from contemporary built architecture and anticipates S. Lorenzo and S. Spirito, in that it has round arches, entablature blocks above the capitals, and an order on the side wall which answers that of the free-standing columns. The resemblance is probably not a coincidence, as Brunelleschi would have often seen the fresco, and as the Temple at Jerusalem was thought of as the prototype for all Christian churches.

63 *The five intercoluminations according to Vitruvius.* The distance between the columns (excluding the thickness of the column) is measured in column-diameters.

64 *The Doric, Ionic and Corinthian orders*, taken from a sixteenth century architectural treatise: Giacomo Barozzi da Vignola, *Regola delli Cinque Ordini d'Architettura*, 1562. These are selected from antique Roman examples and became the canon for most later classical architecture.

65 *S. Pancrazio, portico to the Capella Rucellai.* Not used as a church now, the building abuts on to the back of the Palazzo Rucellai, and was commissioned by Giovanni Rucellai. This portico has now been moved from its original position, and faces onto the street. Compare the intercoluminations with others in this unit.

66 *The Vitruvian temple.* This is a reconstruction, from Vitruvius's description, of the temple he advocated as an ideal. It is basically the same as hundreds built by the Romans in imitation of Greek prototypes.

67 *Vitruvius's Etruscan temple.* This is a reconstruction, from Vitruvius's description, of the Etruscan Temple in Book III, Chapter VII, *De Architectura.* Small Tuscan shrines of this kind have been discovered in recent times.

68 *Alberti's Etruscan temple.* This is a tentative reconstruction of the temple

described in *De Re Aedificatoria*, Book VII, Chapter IV. The description is reproduced in *Holt* (p. 234).

69   *S. Andrea, Mantua.* The black portion of the plan is that part built by Luca Fancelli after Alberti's death (1472–93) according to Alberti's 1470 design. The shaded portion was built much later; the dome was only completed in the eighteenth century.

70   *The Basilica of Maxentius (or Constantine).* Begun 306–12 A.D. under Maxentius and soon completed by Constantine. Its original function was that of a sort of indoor forum, where people could meet in large numbers and judicial proceedings could be held. In the Renaissance, it was in approximately the same state of partial decay as it is now.

71   *A sixteenth-century reconstruction of the plan of the Basilica of Maxentius,* from Serlio, *The Five Books of Architecture,* 1566. The apse on the left has been added for the sake of symmetry; this part of the building was too dilapidated to give Renaissance architects positive information. Originally, there was an entrance porch on this side.

72   *Palazzo Rucellai.* Built by Bernardo Rossellino between 1446 and 1451 on Alberti's designs for Giovanni Rucellai. The façade was built to unify a motley assortment of earlier buildings behind.

73   *Palazzo Rucellai,* Corinthian capital, from the first floor (see Figure 72).

74   *S. Maria Novella, capital.* From the façade. These two capitals were part of Alberti's contribution to the façade (see Figure 32).

75   *The Doric capital,* as described and drawn by Palladio, *The Four Books of Architecture,* 1570, Book I, Chapter XV. Like Vignola, Palladio provided selections of classical details, taken from antiquity, which distilled ideal examples of each order. Alberti advocated and practised this approach, but his examples were on the whole too wayward to achieve consensus agreement.

76   On the left, a reconstruction of the *Doric order* as described by Alberti in Book VII, Chapters VIII and IX. On the right, *Alberti's Doric* from the ground floor of the Palazzo Rucellai (cf. Figure 72).

77   *S. Maria Novella.* Diagram 1 (cf. paragraphs 127–129).

78   *S. Maria Novella.* Diagram 2.

79   *S. Maria Novella.* Diagram 3. (cf. *Wittkower,* pp. 41–7). These diagrams are not precisely to scale, but are meant to elucidate how the various proportional relationships work.

80   *S. Francesco, Rimini* (cf. paragraph 130 and *Wittkower,* p. 37). The half-columns of the ground floor go into the façade three times. The column-diameters go into it approximately twenty-four times. A grid of 'squares' three column-diameters across (eight across and eight high), mark most of the important points vertically and horizontally. This diagram is hypothetical in its details, but the six rectangles (ratio 2 : 3) indicated by the central pair of half-columns fit clearly and logically into the main square and can be seen at a glance.

81   *The Pantheon, Rome.* The dome measures 141 feet across internally. Its massive weight is supported by walls into which huge niches are set, with two columns each to help support the entablature that runs right round the inside of the building. The dome itself is composed of a solid concrete mass reinforced by brick relief arches.

82 A drawing of the *medal struck by Matteo de' Pasti* in 1450 recording
    Alberti's intended façade for S. Francesco, Rimini, with the dome behind
    (cf. *Wittkower*, Plate 15a). Matteo raised the dome on a drum, but this
    may have been to make it more visible, rather than to contradict Alberti's
    intention to make it only as high as it was broad, like the Pantheon.

83 *SS. Annunziata*, Plan. The body of the church was reconstructed between
    1444 and 1481 by Michelozzo and Antonio Manetti. Alberti approved of
    the circular plan of the tribune although a body of opinion considered it
    too pagan.

84 *Roman Triumphal Arch*, based on Alberti's description in *De Re Aedifica-
    toria*, Book VIII, Chapter VI.

85 *Roman Theatre*, based on the description in *De Re Aedificatoria*, Book
    VIII, Chapter VII.

86 *Palazzo Venezia*, Rome, courtyard. At one time this was attributed to
    Alberti, who died in Rome in 1472. The courtyard appears to have been
    built between 1467 and 1471. Conclusive documentary evidence for any
    attribution is lacking, but in several aspects, the courtyard reflects Alberti's
    influence, if not his authorship.

UNIT 10   THREE PROPOSITIONS TOWARDS DEFINING A RENAISSANCE IN 'THE FIGURATIVE ARTS'

142   In the next three units I want to describe and criticize five commonly suggested ways of characterizing the type of changes in Italian painting, and especially in Tuscany, the province around Florence, between, roughly, 1300 and 1520. The five suggested characteristics should enable you to argue about the validity of using the term 'renaissance' to describe this broad period of art history.

I suggest five ways of describing this period's distinguishing changes:
that it was a re-enaction or recreation of the classical style, subject matter and mood (Part 1, Unit 10); that it involved a new way of looking at, and representing, objects and figures, in a naturalistic manner, which happened to involve borrowing certain classical techniques and motifs; that it involved a new relationship between God and man, between man and man, and between a painting and a spectator (Part 2, Unit 10); that it made a significant break with the medieval concentration on religious subject matter and became more secular in its choice (Unit 11); and finally, that it is characterized by the appearance of a new type of artist, conscious of his individual role in the history of art, and claiming new status and new power for himself and therefore, for art (Unit 12).

143   This unit deals with the first three of these definitions of a 'renaissance' in painting in Tuscany. Unit 11, which deals with the meaning of paintings and sculptures will treat the fourth definition. Unit 12, which describes the development of artistic status during this period will deal with the fifth definition. At the end you can come to some conclusions about the compatibility of these definitions and the way they affect any decisions about when, where, why and how a 'renaissance' happened. You should already have noted that the list of definitions reflects arguments about the whole period – in their stress on individualism, naturalism, and on secularization, so you should remember criticisms which have already been discussed with reference to these type of statements, as you read.

Contents

144   The unit is divided into two parts. The first deals with the argument that Renaissance art, especially painting, was the result of interest in classicism; the second with the suggestion that it was rather, the development of a new style based on interest in realism.

Part 1   Proposition (i)   The Renaissance in painting consisted of a recreation of classical styles, subject matter and mood.
Proposition (ii)   This classical Renaissance began in Tuscany in the early fourteenth century.
Proposition (iii)   The fifteenth-century recreation of classicism in Tuscany was successful.
Proposition (iv)   Interest in classical art changed radically in the fifteenth century.
Part 2   Proposition (i)   The phenomena of Florentine painting between about 1300 and 1520 is best explained as the development of a new style based on interest in realism.

Proposition (ii) This development was not consistent throughout the period 1300–1520.

Proposition (iii) Realism in art was related to the growth of a sense of intimacy between man and God.

Proposition (iv) For Renaissance painters realism did not mean painting what they saw.

(a) Fidelity to Nature versus tradition and the problems of creating a 'slice of life'.

(b) Fidelity to Nature and teaching the illiterate.

(c) Fidelity to Nature and an Ideal of beauty.

Plates and Figures for Unit 10

PLATES

1 *The Mysteries, fresco*, Pompei, first century B.C. (*Scala*).
2 *Genesis scenes*, Moutier-Grandval Bible, Tours, 834–43 (*British Museum*).
3 *The Expulsion of the Traders from the Temple*, Giotto, *fresco*, Arena chapel, Padua, *c.* 1303 (*Scala*).
4 *St. Francis before the Sultan*, Giotto, *fresco*, S. Francesco, Assisi, *c.* 1303 (*Kunsthistorisches Museum, Vienna*).
5 *The Trinity with St. John, the Virgin and Donors*, Masaccio, *fresco*, Santa Maria Novella, Florence, 1425–7 (*Scala*).
6 *The Aeneid*, Apollonio di Giovanni, panel of a wedding chest, Courtauld Institute Gallery, *c.* 1460.
7 *The Baptism of Christ*, Piero della Francesca (*National Gallery*).
8 *The Nativity*, Piero della Francesca (*National Gallery*).
9 *The Martyrdom of San Sebastian*, Pollaiuolo, 1475? (*National Gallery*).

FIGURES

87 *The Poets on Parnassus*, Raphael, *fresco*, Stanza della Segnatura, Vatican, *c.* 1509 (*Mansell Collection*).
88 *The Three Graces, fresco*, Pompei (*Mansell Collection*).
89 *The Odyssey*, Roman wall painting, Museo Profano, Vatican (*Mansell Collection*).
90 *The Entry into Jerusalem* from the Gospelbook of Otto III, *c.* 1000 (MS. No. CLM 4453 f. 234v.) (*Bavarian State Library*).
91 *St. Mark*, The Gospels of Charlemagne, Vienna, early ninth century (*Scala*).
92 *A Wingèd Fame*, Roman, Pinacotheca, Siena (*Mansell Collection*).
93 *Securitas* in *Good Government in the Country*, Ambrogio Lorenzetti, *fresco*, Sala delle Pace, Palazzo Publico, Siena, 1338–9 (*Mansell Collection*).
94 *The Lamentation*, Giotto, *fresco*, Arena Chapel, Padua, *c.* 1306 (*Mansell Collection*).
95 *Meleager's death*, Roman sarcophagus (*Louvre*).
96 *The First page of Petrarch's copy of Vergil*, Simone Martini, Bibliotheca Ambrosiana Milan, *c.* 1340.
97 *The Expulsion of the Traders from the Temple*, mosaic, Monreale Sicily, twelfth century (*Mansell Collection*).
98 Abraham and the angels – from Barberini's copies of Cavallini (Vat. Barb. Lat. 4406, f36) (*Biblioteca Apostolica Vaticana, Rome*).
99 *Gemini*, Aratus MS. University Library, Leiden, 800–50.
100 *Last Judgement*, Utrecht Psalter, (Cod. 32 fol. 48v.), *University of Utrecht*, 820–30.
101 *Prudence*, Giovanni Pisano, marble, The Pulpit, Pisa Cathedral, 1302 (*Mansell Collection*).
102 *A Maenad*, Museo Nuovo nel Palazzo dei Conservatori, Rome (*Mansell Collection*).
103 *Dancing Nudes*, Pollaiuolo, *fresco*, Villa Arcetri, Florence (*Mansell Collection*).
104 *Hercules fighting the Hydra*, Pollaiuolo, Uffizi, Florence, 1465–70 (*Mansell Collection*).
105 *The Three Graces*, Raphael, Musée Condé Chantilly, 1502–3 (*Giraudon*).
106 *The Three Graces*, from *The Praise of Robert of Anjou* by Convenevole da Prato, Vienna, *c.* 1340 (*Austrian National Library*).
107 *The Three Graces*, Roman, Libreria Piccolomini, Siena (*Mansell Collection*).
108 *The Disputà*, Raphael, *fresco*, Stanza della Segnatura, Vatican, *c.* 1509 (*Mansell Collection*).
109 *The Maestà*, Duccio, Museo del Opera del Duomo, Siena, 1308–11 (*Mansell Collection*).

110   *The Madonna of Humility*, Workshop of Simone Martini, Kaiser Friedrich Museum, Berlin, *c.* 1330.

111   *The Madonna of Humility*, follower of Nardo, Academy, Florence, *c.* 1360 (*Mansell Collection*).

112   *St. Francis receiving confirmation of his rule*, Ghirlandaio, Sassetti Chapel, S. Trinità, Florence, 1484–6 (*Mansell Collection*).

113   *St. Francis resuscitating a boy of the Spini family*, Ghirlandaio, Sassetti Chapel, S. Trinità, Florence, 1484–6 (*Mansell Collection*).

114   Preparatory drawing for Figure 112, Ghirlandaio (*Kupferstichkabinett, Berlin*).

115   *The Flood*, Paolo Uccello, *fresco*, formerly in the Chiostre Verde, S. Maria Novella, Florence, *c.* 1431 (*Scala*).

116   *The Apotheosis of St. Thomas Aquinas*, Andrea de Firenze, *fresco*, The Spanish Chapel, S. Maria Novella, Florence, *c.* 1360 (*Mansell Collection*).

117   *The Attempt to destroy the Host*, Paolo Uccello, Galleria Nazionale delle Marche, Urbino, 1465 (*Mansell Collection*).

PART 1 PROPOSITION (i) THE RENAISSANCE IN PAINTING CONSISTED OF A RE-ENACTION OR RECREATION OF CLASSICAL STYLES, MOOD AND SUBJECT MATTER

145   The basic implication of the term 'Renaissance' is that it meant a 'rebirth' of classicism in art. Compare *A scene from the Villa of the Mysteries* (from now on referred to as *The Mysteries*) (Plate 1) painted at Pompeii in the first century A.D. and *Parnassus* (Figure 87), painted around 1509, in Rome, by the painter Raphael. Pause, and ask yourself how thorough Raphael's recreation of classical art was, and whether the sympathy between the two paintings is extraordinary. Because Raphael had not, in fact, seen any classical paintings like this. Can you see any similarities in subject, form, costume or mood?

146   Raphael has treated a classical subject (the poets on Parnassus headed by Apollo and the Nine Muses) in classical form (note the sense of solidity and liveliness in each figure, the use of relief-modelling and the clear sense of space), in classical costume, and, most important though perhaps most evasive, in a classical mood, by which I mean a pervasive equilibrium and tranquillity. Raphael has produced what is not a copy of any particular classical painting, but a classical production in its own right. And this is very extraordinary, because the two paintings were produced in cultures widely differing from one another, and they are separated by fifteen hundred years, during which the principles of classical art were neglected either partially or wholly.

147   How did Raphael achieve his recreation? Since a complete recreation of classical painting involves the assimilation of its forms, subject matter and mood, when did this happen, or did it ever really happen at all? Before answering such questions you must get a clear idea of some of the specific characteristics of classical painting, so that you can gauge its influence on later painting.

148   In the two columns below I have prepared a tabulated comparison between classical and medieval painting. The examples of classical painting are:
The Mysteries (Plate 1); first century A.D.;
The Three Graces (Figure 88) and a Roman wall-painting of a scene from the Odyssey (now referred to as *The Odyssey* (Figure 89). The examples of medieval painting are:

The Genesis Scenes (Plate 2) from the Moutier-Grandval Bible, Tours, 834–843;
The Entry into Jerusalem (Figure 90) from Henry II's Sacramentary, 1002–1014.

The classical examples are all wall-paintings. The medieval paintings are all small, as they come from books. This is typical though there are, of course, medieval wall-paintings. In my tabulation, I've muddled various statements, placing them in the wrong columns. They are all numbered and are arranged in pairs of 'opposites', so after you have read them carefully, and compared them with the illustrations, fill in the model tabulation on page 92, with the right numbers in the right columns.

CLASSICAL PLATE 1, FIGURES 88, 89	MEDIEVAL PLATE 2, FIGURE 90
1 The painting surface is opaque. There is little attempt to deny the two-dimensional surface on which one knows the figures are painted.	2 The painting surface is transparent. You look through it into the emphatically three-dimensional world 'beyond' as if it were a window.
3 The figures and objects appear to stand on a floor on which the spectator could walk.	4 The figures and objects are applied on to a flat surface parallel to the spectator, or stand on a line or narrow shelf which seems to slant uphill.
5 The picture creates a spacious world inhabited by volumetric bodies, which appear to have freedom of movement, similar to the spectator's own. The figures and objects are modelled in light and shade (hence their 'relief' or three-dimensional solidity). They vary in size depending on whether they are imagined to be near or far from the spectator.	6 The figures and objects are delineated with firm lines, and do not appear to inhabit a space in which, or into which the spectator could himself walk. They vary in size depending on their symbolic importance in the picture, or their decorative balance.
7 Ground and figures are separated from one another. Sometimes figures are overlapped but the depth is shallow and often crowded, or recedes in jolts from foreground to background.	8 A sense of depth is achieved by making parallel lines converge, by shrinking the size of objects in the distance, by overlapping shapes so that one 'is' behind the other and by blurring definition and colour in the 'distance'.
9 Figures do not seem capable of movement, or move across the surface of the painting.	10 Figures gesture and move in and out of imagined space as well as across it.
11 Figures turn their backs on the spectator or face directly out to him, as well as being engrossed in one another. This is part of the invitation to the spectator to 'enter into' the picture physically and emotionally.	12 Figures are usually either frontal or in profile. Though bodies may twist, the twist is not organically handled. The aim of the picture is not to get the spectator to imagine what a figure with its back turned feels or looks like.

13   The painting tells a story, or more often expresses an idea, by the use of symbols and symbolic colours, as well as the symbolic placing of figures and objects in the design.

14   The scene tells a story through engaging the spectator in personal sympathy with the actions and re-actions of individual figures. Faces and figures therefore are often highly individualized, in a dramatic event.

15   The aim is to capture a specific psychological and physical moment. This is present even in landscape, where sky and earth are caught at an instant of a particular type of weather.

16   The aim is to express a timeless idea, even in portraying an event.

17   The emotions of figures are con-ventionalized, or pressed into the shapes of drapery, composition, or various hues, to pervade the whole design. Otherwise, colour is sum-mary, i.e. blue for the sea, green for grass, etc. . .

18   Emotions are conveyed by speci-fic gestures and facial expressions are individualized. Colouring is often subtle, and rarely uniform over any large area. It attempts to match the subtleties and variations in nature.

19   The spectator is encouraged to enter into the pictured event because figures often invite him with a glance or gesture, and their 'space' seems traversable to him.

20   The spectator becomes engrossed in the painting, spurred by the abstract effects of colour and pattern, or by the way he recognizes certain symbols with all their emotional and intellectual references.

21   The spectator is directly pro-vided with the idea or subject matter of the picture, through symbols and so on. He must intuit for himself the specific human expressions or feelings of figures involved in the event.

22   The spectator is provided with detailed information about the feel-ings and thoughts of the participants in the painting. He must interpret the idea behind the painting from these 'clues'.

Figure 87

Figure 88

Figure 89

Figure 90

TEST BOX

Classical	Medieval

SPECIMEN ANSWER

Classical	Medieval
2	1
3	4
5	6
8	7
10	9
11	12
14	13
15	16
18	17
19	20
22	21

49   Naturally, this comparison has been extremely sweeping, but it is very important at this stage to draw a clear distinction between classical and medieval art, even though you may want to modify it quite a lot later. So I shall permit myself some more sweeping comparisons. Naturally the medieval paintings all treat Christian subjects, and the classical treat Roman religious topics or illustrate classical literature (though medieval artists did illustrate classical literature). Let me sum up by saying, that while classical art conveys real or supernatural events in terms of every day human experience of time and space, medieval painting treats the real and the supernatural in terms of a time and space unlike the common-sense world.

50   There are in fact some other more technical features which historians look for when they want to gauge classical influence in a painting. They are: the appearance of types of classical ornament or architecture which you have seen in Unit 9; the use of classical subject matter like that dealt with in Units 5–6 and with which Unit 11, *Iconography*, deals; the use of types of classical drapery or costume (for when medieval artists painted classical figures they dressed them in medieval contemporary costume) and the appearance of techniques, like *fresco* in painting or drilling in sculpture. But their recognition is more of a specialist matter. Finally, medieval painting only depicted the nude body where it was absolutely essential, as in *The Creation*, whereas Roman painters used the nude in many subjects.

Proposition (ii)   The Classical Renaissance began in Tuscany in the early fourteenth century

51   Before reading on, read a passage from *Holt* (pp. 152–4). When did Ghiberti think the new style in art had begun?

For many generations scholars have agreed with Ghiberti that the style of Giotto, Cimabue and their contemporaries in the late thirteenth and early fourteenth centuries represents the beginning of a new type of art. Did this break-through involve the recreation of classical art? Compare *The Expulsion of the Traders from the Temple*, painted in *fresco*, by Giotto in the Arena Chapel in Padua (Plate 3) and the three examples of classical paintings you've already examined (Plate 1, Figures 88, 89). Can you see similarities between Giotto's work and the classical paintings?

152 The subject of Giotto's painting isn't classical. It is Christian. There are no nudes in his painting, and no use of distant landscape. But Giotto has modelled his figures and objects with light and shade, so that they appear substantial and volumetric. He's put them in a reasonably deep space framed by an architectural setting with little pillars with classical capitals. His painting is of a narrative seen through a 'window'. It tells a story through representing the feelings and actions of the characters in a drama. To the left, the Apostles watch Christ dismissing two protesting traders and their sheep, birds and bullocks. To the right a group of Pharisees mutter disparagingly. There's a little child holding a bird in front of one of the Apostles. He invites the spectator to share the experience of the scene rather as the figure in *The Mysteries* (Plate 1) who looks out at the spectator. The pharisee to the far right is important too. His face is hidden behind his companion, daring the spectator not to believe in the spaciousness of the scene! These two figures especially, emphasize how far Giotto had departed from the traditions of medieval art.

153 Giotto and his contemporaries did actually sometimes quote an entire classical figure in their pictures. In *St. Francis before the Sultan* by Giotto (Plate 4) try to recognize the 'quotation', and try to guess its justification in a Christian painting. Remember that the Sultan was an enemy of Christianity.

Giotto quoted some classical cupids in the little statues that decorate the building on the left. But he had to have an excuse for them. His excuse was probably that pagan statues (for that was how medieval theologians regarded classical art) symbolized the enmity of the Sultan to the Church. Note too, that the cupids are statues only, not 'alive' in the picture. Cimabue, in his paintings in the Upper Church of Assisi, could use classical acanthus ornament in the borders separating his scenes. The Sienese painter, Ambrogio Lorenzetti, could copy a Roman sculpture for his figure of Security (Figures 92, 93), but this was used as part of a deeply symbolic Christian allegory of *Good Government*. Giotto adapted the figure of a mourner in a sarcophagus representing the death of Meleager for his depiction of the grief-stricken St. John in his *Lamentation* (Figures 94, 95). In this picture, Giotto adopted the classical convention of representing some figures with their backs turned to the spectator. It's very important, however, to realize that such quotations were either carefully Christianized or were already 'neutral', like ornaments, and we often do not know their exact sources.

154 Now look at Simone Martini's depiction of Vergil, for the first page of Petrarch's copy of Vergil's work (Figure 96). Does it suggest another characteristic of this generation's attitude to classicism?

Figure 91

Figure 92

Figure 93

Simone has clothed Vergil in contemporary costume and put him in a Gothic meadow. Not even Petrarch was really conscious of the difference between his own culture and that of Rome. Vergil was, in fact, often thought of as a sort of prophet of Christianity and treated as though he were a medieval poet. Remember that Dante was guided by Vergil in the *Divine Comedy*. Similarly, historians still regarded their society, and the Holy Roman Empire as a continuation of the Roman Empire. But you can't *reconstruct* a style until you understand that you must self-consciously elide those facets of your style which are different from the one you wish to copy. This self-consciousness didn't emerge until well into the fifteenth century in Florence, as will be explained in Proposition (iv).

155 Perhaps the only genuinely classical revival of the early fourteenth century was that of *fresco*, which is the medium of *The Mysteries* (Plate 1). *Fresco*, which means painting on *fresh*, wet plaster with pigments mixed with water, is the medium of nearly all the great painters of Tuscany, including Michelangelo. Medieval painting was often on a very small scale and easily portable. Large-scale wall decoration in Italy had always been done in mosaic (which was, of course, a classical medium too!) or *secco* (that is painting on a dry wall). But the popularity of *fresco* meant that painting again became a large-scale medium. It has another more important consequence too. Compare Giotto's *Expulsion of the Traders from the Temple* (Plate 3), painted in *fresco*, with a mosaic of the same subject, from Monreale in Sicily, executed about a century earlier (Figure 97). What is the difference between the two media? Could Giotto have created his painting in mosaic? The basic units of mosaic work are little coloured squares of stone and glass.

156 The basic units of *fresco* are brush-strokes, which can be made broad or thin, and loaded with paint mixed to a desired colour. Being more uniform in size and colour, it is more difficult for the mosaic worker to use the little stones of mosaic to achieve the sort of subtle modelling with gradations of tone on which the 'window' effect in painting depends. For instance, in mosaic you can't characterize the subtleties of a facial expression, or indeed the softness of skin or cloth, as minutely as you can in paint. The difference between painting on a dry wall, and painting in *fresco* is not important here, but there is a television programme in week 13 which deals with this topic.

157 Why did Giotto's generation revive the medium of *fresco* at all? Added to the fact that it enabled them to create a 'window' painting, it has been suggested that *fresco* was much cheaper and quicker than mosaic work. Perhaps it met the demands of the new patrons – the increasingly prosperous communes, and the new Franciscan and Dominican orders – more easily. A more direct precondition of the revival however, was probably the fact that a painter called Pietro Cavallini in the late thirteenth century reconstructed some Early Christian frescoes in the Roman church of *S. Paolo Fuori la mura* and then painted frescoes himself in *S. Cecilia del Trastevere* and at *S. Francesco* in Assisi (Figure 98). Why *did* Giotto and his generation need to copy copies of Early Christian (that is Late Roman) paintings if they wanted to be classical? The amazing fact is, that a painter like Giotto, or even Raphael for that matter, had *never* seen classical painting of remotely the quality of *The Mysteries*, *The Three Graces*, or *The Odyssey Landscape*. The paintings of Herculaneum and of Pompei, which are our main source of knowledge about classical painting, were not excavated until the eighteenth century. In what form then, was

classical art available to the artists of the early fourteenth century? Remember the sources I've already described and make a brief list of them. Then try to guess what sort of classical objects might survive a thousand years among cultures often hostile to them.

Figure 94

Figure 95

Figure 96

158   The sources I have mentioned are relief sarcophagi, architectural ornament,
and late Roman murals in Christian churches. The survival of classical art
was very patchy. Some figure sculpture in the round did survive, and stone
sculpture, especially reliefs on heavy sarcophagi survived better than other
media. Sculpture had often been incorporated into buildings, simply as
masonry, and the really heavy pieces had been too big to break up in the
iconoclastic purges of the Early Church. Naturally, bronze sculpture had often
been melted down. Paintings and mosaics were buried deep underground in
Roman houses or temples by the fourteenth century, except where they were
in Christian churches. So the remains of classical art, until purposeful ex-
cavation got under way, were rather battered and often of poor workmanship,
for the statues were copies of copies themselves and the sarcophagi often
mass-produced in Roman workshops. Or they were very small, like the coins
and engraved gems that were collected in monastic treasuries. Or like the
Early Christian murals of churches and catacombs they rarely represented the
high point of classical art. What survived best was sculpture, so a fourteenth-
century painter had to translate a figure or an effect into another medium.
Perhaps this explains the great advantage the sculptors of the fourteenth and
fifteenth century had over painters. Certainly sculptors took the lead in
assimilating classicism. It is important to realize however, that more classical
art was available in Italy than elsewhere and this gave Italy a privileged
position.

159   Classical influence survived in another way. It was 'carried' by Byzantine art.
Look again at the mosaic of *The Expulsion of the Traders from the Temple* from
Monreale in Sicily (Figure 97). Try to pick out classical features in it. Then
read some passages from *Holt* (pp. 8–9, 13). Did Italians like Byzantine art?

Figure 97

Figure 98

The perspective space in the mosaic is rather odd and the figures do vary in size according to their symbolic significance, but the scene does represent an event – an action, and it does attempt perspective depth and human drama. You will have gathered too, from the extract you read, that Byzantine art was admired in the twelfth century in Italy and that young Italian artists were being taught its skills.

60   Classical art survived in classical objects, and in other artistic styles. It was also periodically revived throughout the Middle Ages. There were, in fact, several 'renaissances' before the Renaissance, among them one in Rome in the sixth century; in the ninth century in Carolingian France, and one in the twelfth century again in France. How thorough were such revivals? Let's examine some examples of the Carolingian Renaissance, which lasted briefly while the Emperor Charlemagne attempted to revive both the institutions and the culture of the Roman Empire: *St. Mark*, from The Gospels of Charlemagne (Figure 91): *The Gemini of the Zodiac* from the Aratus Ms (a Stoic poem

with astrological interest) (Figure 99); a page from the *Utrecht Psalter* illustrating the Last Judgement (Figure 100). Which seems most similar to classical Roman art? The art of Giotto and his contemporaries, or these three works from Carolingian France?

Figure 99

161   The figures of Gemini (Figure 99) represent nude personifications of a Zodiacal sign in thoroughly classical fashion with none of the self-consciousness or prudery which characterized the medieval and fourteenth-century approach to the nude body. Nor is it a symbol of Christian virtue or pagan vice. It is classical in meaning and form. Although the landscape and figures of the *Utrecht Psalter* (Figure 100) have no definite sense of spatial relationships, they approximate much closer to the airy, weather-filled landscape and active little figures of *The Odyssey Landscape* (Figure 89) than the sort of landscape Lorenzetti produced in his *Good Government in the Country* (Figure 93). *St. Mark* however (Figure 91) reminds one equally of Giotto's work, and *The Mysteries* (Plate 1). All these 'renaissances' petered out, but they meant that new sources of classicism were injected into European art. It is typical that when humanists came to revive 'good' Roman script, they used Carolingian models. In fact, both you and I write in Carolingian script ourselves. The very eclecticism of classical sources which fourteenth- and fifteenth-century painters used, meant that it is usually better to say that a painting is in an 'antique' manner, than in a 'classical' manner, as classical in this period does not usually have the well-defined meaning we use, and 'antique' is a better 'umbrella' word for the variety of sources used.

162   All Christian art, *without exception*, was always saturated in classical elements, though these were often a matter of symbolic motifs or compositional designs. Christ and his Apostles are dressed in togas, because Early Christian painters modelled their representation on classical ways of depicting Philosophers. Christ as the Good Shepherd derives from scenes of the Orpheus cult. The Madonna and Child depends on pagan, Roman representations of the Childhood of Dionysos. It is very important to realize that when Christian sculptors and painters found classical reliefs, they often found elements which were already familiar to them and therefore sympathetic to their needs, because they were looking at designs or motifs which were, however remotely, still present in their art.

Figure 100

163 It was important too, that Italy had always remained a relative back water to the great movements of medieval art, which originated in the North, and always retained more classical elements in its art, because Italy had never been 'taken over' completely, by Northern styles. For instance, Italian churches never succumbed to the Gothic habit, so popular in Northern France and England, of breaking a wall up into huge areas of stained glass or into sculptural decoration. Mosaics had always been the traditional medieval Italian decoration for church walls. So, when *fresco* appeared, it was well suited to Italian building styles. Renaissances previous to the one in the early fourteenth century in Tuscany were not successful and you've seen that in many ways the Carolingian revival of classicism was *more* thorough than that of Giotto and his contemporaries. Was Giotto's 'renaissance' successful either? By which I mean, did a revival of classicism develop consistently from the time of Giotto and Lorenzetti in the early fourteenth century to the time of Raphael and Michelangelo in the sixteenth century? I want you to examine some evidence in order to decide this question.

164 Probably in 1334 in Siena a Roman statue was discovered by chance when a fountain was being made. It may have been of Venus. I want you to read more about its discovery and its final fate in 1357 in the words of the sculptor Ghiberti, writing about eighty years later. The passage comes from *Holt*, pp. 165–6. Look too at the differences between a painting of the 1300s (Plate 3) and one of the 1360s (Figure 116). The next evidence we have of anyone taking interest in classical sculpture is in a comment by an early humanist called Giovanni Dondi, who wrote in 1375 or so that there were artists obsessed and amazed by 'the better-than-nature sculpture of the ancients' and he seemed rather surprised about it. What conclusions would you draw about the progress of the 'Renaissance' from all this evidence?

101

There was obviously a hiatus in the 'Renaissance' between about 1340 and 1370 or even later, in Tuscany. From your knowledge of Florentine history during this period, particularly what you know from reading Brucker's book and Unit 7 by John Larner, could you guess what caused and characterized this hiatus?

165   You should have remembered that Florence suffered both the Plague and a terrible economic recession during just this period. The peace, political stability and prosperity of the early fourteenth century, which seems to be connected with a more humane and relaxed religious outlook and a delight in paintings quoting classical motifs and representing God among men, taking part in everyday events, crumbled. In his book *Painting in Florence and Siena after the Black Death*, Meillard Meiss explained this hiatus as the result of changed economic and social conditions. He explains that the artists and patrons who admired Giotto's and Lorenzetti's work either died or were ruined economically. In their place came a different type of artist like Andrea da Firenze (Figure 116) catering for the new patrons thrown up from a more conservative class of businessmen or moving from the more old-fashioned country areas to the towns. The public, harassed by double disaster, revolted against the style of Giotto and returned briefly to the more remote, symbolic and hieratic style of the thirteenth century. All classicism was again thought pagan, irreligious and as in Siena in 1357, dangerous – the symbol of loose living.

Figures 101 and 102

Proposition (iii) The fifteenth-century recreation of classicism was successful

66 When you read Peter and Linda Murray's *The Art of the Renaissance*, you will find that it begins not with Giotto, but with Masaccio, who painted in the 1420s in Florence, and died very young at twenty-six in 1428. Read what Alberti, the great art theorist of the fifteenth century, said about the 'revival' of art in *Holt*, (pp. 205–6). When did Alberti think a revival had begun and to what did he attribute it?

Alberti singles out five contemporary artists, Luca della Robbia, Donatello and Ghiberti, who were sculptors, Brunelleschi, the architect, and Masaccio, as men who represented a revival of talent which he equates with, but *does not* attribute to, classical art. In fact, he thinks, because these artists had so little guidance, they are especially praiseworthy.

67 How far do *you* think classicism contributed to Masaccio's style? Was his classicism different from Giotto's? Examine Masaccio's *Trinity, The Virgin, St. John and Donors* (Plate 5), *Adam and Eve driven from Paradise* (*Murray*, Figure 40), and a sculpture of *Prudence* modelled in 1302 on classical sculpture of the Venus Pudica by Giovanni Pisano (Figure 101).

Masaccio has handled the nude body with great subtlety and dignity. He uses it, as classical artists had done, to convey the most noble and intimate mental states. Like his nudes, his classical architectural setting is much more accurate than Giotto's. But Masaccio, like Giotto, still uses the nude only where it was conventional to do so, as in a Genesis scene. He didn't paint classical stories or subjects (perhaps because he was not asked to). He placed religious events against classical backgrounds without feeling the need to adapt figures to buildings, though, of course, Masaccio makes the juxtaposition 'seem' absolutely right. His figures have relatively classical proportions and take up complex poses turning in and out of space, but for him, classicism is still in the service of Christian themes. It's typical too, that Masaccio seems to have derived his figure of Eve, not directly from a classical course, but through the work of a Tuscan sculptor. At this period, painting lagged behind sculpture in its assimilation of classical forms. You've probably guessed too that Masaccio gained his knowledge of classical architecture through Brunelleschi. He repeats Brunelleschi's mistaken reconstruction of a Roman barrel vault. He gives the divisions of the vault an even number (so that a rib of stone, like that of a Gothic rib vault centres over Christ's head) rather than the correct odd number.

68 To make paintings look more classical artists had to illustrate classical stories in a classical style, they had to stop placing figures in contemporary costumes in classical buildings, and they had to use classical conventions for conveying vivacity and movement, as well as volume and space in painting. When did these three things happen? What are the differences between Mantegna's

St. James led to Execution (*Murray*, 109), painted in Padua in 1455 and Apollonio di Giovanni's scene from *The Aeneid*, painted in Florence in the 1460s (Plate 6)?

St. James had been a Roman martyr, so Mantegna dressed his figures in classical costume and put them in a classical building full of reliefs and inscriptions. Apollonio had a classical subject too, but he made his scene like a Florentine tournament, full of bright colours and little courtiers inhabiting the Capitol in Rome. In fact it was not in Florence that artists began to harmonize classical architectural settings with classical figures. It was in Padua, perhaps because this city was a great centre for archaeological studies.

169   But Mantegna's painting still lacks other classical constituents which Florentine sculptors had already grasped. Pin-point these 'deficiencies' by comparing Mantegna's picture with Donatello's *St. George and the Dragon* (*Murray*, Figure 25), and a Graeco-Roman relief of *A Maenad* (Figure 102). Read Vasari's criticism of Mantegna's work:

> . . . it was his [Mantegna's] theory, confirmed by what he saw with his own eyes, that the sculptors of the ancient world had used several living models to create the perfection and beauty which nature rarely brings together in a single form: they found it necessary to take one part from one body and another from another. As well as this, the statues he copied seemed to Andrea, to be more detailed and clearly defined as regards the muscles, veins, nerves, and so forth which nature conceals with a soft covering of flesh, except in the case of the old or the emaciated whom artists anyhow for other reasons will not use as models. Andrea's fondness for this theory can be seen in his works, whose style is in fact quite sharp and sometimes suggests stone rather than living flesh.
>
> *Vasari: The Lives of the Artists*, trans. G. Bull, 1965, p. 243 (from now on, referred to merely as 'Vasari').

Figure 103

Figure 104

Figure 105

Figure 106

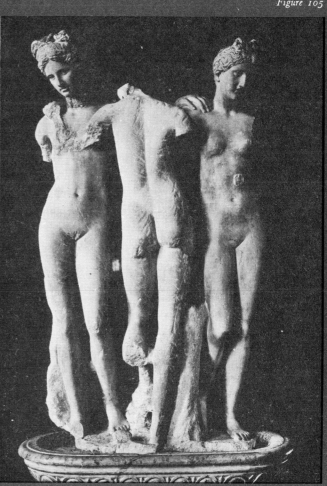

Figure 107

Vasari says that Mantegna made his figures look as though they were made of stone. This highlights the fact that both Donatello and the Graeco-Roman sculptor achieved a tremendous feeling of liveliness and airiness of movement in stone reliefs. It's a vivacity and sense of the instantaneous conveyed largely by an emphasis on the motifs of fluttering hair and drapery and the twisted poses. These elements suggest restless movement, air or wind blowing against figures and the sort of delicate balance hinting at continuous motion. Alberti had, in fact, recommended these motifs to painters in 1435, but they did not take up his suggestion until about a generation later.

> The body is said to live when it has certain voluntary movements. It is said to be dead when the members no longer are able to carry on the functions of life, that is, movement and feeling. Therefore the painter, wishing to express life in things, will make every part in motion – but in motion he will keep loveliness and grace. The most graceful movements and the most lively are those which move upwards into the air. . . . I am delighted to see some movement in hair, locks of hair, branches, fronds and robes. . . . movements are especially pleasing in hair where part of it turns in spirals as if wishing to knot itself, waves in the air like flames, twines around itself like a serpent, while part rises here, part there. In the same way branches twist themselves now up, now down, now away, now near, the parts contorting themselves like ropes. Folds act in the same way, emerging like the branches from the trunk of a tree. . . . no part of the cloth is bare of movement. As I have noted, movements should be moderated and sweet. They should appear graceful to the observer rather than a marvel of study. However, where we should like to find movement in the draperies, cloth is by nature heavy and falls to the earth. For this reason it would be well to place in the picture the face of the wind Zephyrus or Austrus who blows from the clouds making the draperies move in the wind. Thus you will see with what grace the bodies, where they are struck by the wind, show the nude under the draperies in suitable parts. In the other parts the draperies blown by the wind fly gracefully through the air. In this blowing in the wind the painter should take care not to display any drape against the wind.
>
> From *On Painting* by L. B. Alberti, trans. J. R. Spencer, Yale University Press, 1966 (from now on referred to as 'Alberti') pp. 74–81.

170   Giotto and Masaccio were intent, as Vasari says in the Life of Masaccio, on making their figures seem to stand firmly on the ground. They wanted to give them solid existence in *credible* space, rather than floating in the 'supernatural' time and space of medieval painting. Like them, Mantegna still indicated depth by a mesh of perspective lines, by placing objects 'in front' of one another and by volumetric modelling in light and shade. The result in all these painters' work is a great dignity and grandeur which has often been called epic, but this gravity (in both senses) probably seemed rather stolid to painters of the last quarter of the fifteenth century in Florence. Look at Pollaiuolo's *Dancing Nudes* and *Hercules fighting the Hydra* (Figures 103, 104) and at Botticelli's *Spring* (*Murray*, Figure 1). How do these painters create a sense of depth, mass and human action?

171   In Pollaiuolo's cavorting and fierce nudes, and in Botticelli's willowy figures surrounded by billowing hair and drapery, it's easy to see that painters had begun to follow Alberti's advice and the example of sculptors of the previous generation. Depth is not indicated by perspective *lines*, or solely by careful relief modelling. Rather, an airy and open spaciousness is presupposed by the freedom of movement in the figures – setting the spectator to accept the delicate graduation of tone in the landscape, or even, a blank background, as in Pollaiuolo's *Dancing Nudes*, as depth. Perhaps it was not until artists like Masaccio, Mantegna and Giotto had reacted against the spatial ambi-

guity of medieval art by their close attention to careful placing of mass and space, that Pollaiuolo or Botticelli could again, but with totally different effect, set their figures free in a looser, more imagined space, or dare to 'leave out' perspective lines. Masaccio and Giotto clung to the architectural settings which hold figures in space. It was perhaps, not until the spectator had been 'educated' to expect and accept this sort of realism, that an artist like Botticelli could abandon 'building space' with its plain surfaces, and set figures in the flickering, highly varied textures of landscape. And, of course, the 'ambience' of landscape, (which is related to classical influence only in so far as artists had read about classical landscapes) contributes so much to the liveliness of Botticelli's or Pollaiuolo's figures.

72   Yet in one specific way, both Pollaiuolo and Botticelli, like Mantegna, lack certain classical elements which Giotto and Masaccio possessed. Read this passage from Alberti's *On Painting* and decide what they might be.

> I say that in this circumscription one ought to take great pains to make these lines so fine that they can scarcely be seen. The painter Apelles used to practise this and to compete with Protogenes. Because circumscription is nothing but the drawing of the outline, which when done with too apparent a line does not indicate a margin of the plane but a neat cleavage, I should desire that only the movement of the outline be inscribed.
>
> Alberti, p. 68.

Mantegna, Botticelli and Pollaiuolo define shape with a sinuous and wiry line. In Mantegna this is perhaps the product of his antiquarian interest in defining classical detail as Vasari stresses. In the other two painters the interest in decorative linear pattern may be a counterpart to the twisted and complex shapes of figures, hair and drapery they had adopted. What is interesting, is that the sinuous line, intensive detail and decorative pattern act against just those principles of vivacity, movement and airy depth in figures and landscape which were new to Florentine painting. As Alberti says 'too apparent a line' creates 'a neat cleavage'. Neat lines, in fact, flatten forms and pin them down, in defining them. This is why Masaccio and Giotto, though their figures are very still, create a strong sense of depth, mass and life. Their figures are subtly modelled in gradations of tones, not really *delineated*. The very neatness of Botticelli's or Pollaiuolo's work also seem to prevent them from suggesting movement by the rapid and careless method Alberti recommends.

> Who could ever without the greatest study express faces in which mouth, chin, eyes, cheeks, forehead and eyebrows all were in harmony with laughter or weeping. For this reason it is best to learn them from nature and always to do these things very rapidly, letting the observer think he sees more than he actually sees.
>
> Alberti, p. 78.

It is only in the paintings of the sixteenth century (except in Leonardo's work as will be explained in Unit 13) that this suggestion of leaving something to the spectator's imagination is adopted. Now look at Raphael's *Parnassus* (Figure 87). Has Raphael somehow struck a balance between movement and solidity, airy space and mass, line and light and shade? I think he has, and I think this 'balance' is what makes his paintings like *The Dionysiac Mysteries* in form, and in mood. But you will be aware by now, that Raphael acquired this classical combination of suggestion and definition, movement and calm through developments often unconnected with direct copying of classical painting.

Proposition (iv)   Interest in classical art changed radically during the fifteenth century

EXERCISE

173 I want you to examine some pictures, sculptures and quotations. After you have done so, suggest factors affecting the assimilation of classicism by artists in Florence, in the fifteenth and, especially, the sixteenth century.

1 Read the following passages from *Holt:* pages 166–7; 176–9; 289–96.

2 In 1464, the painter Mantegna and his humanist friends (including the antiquarian Felice Feliciano), dressed up in wreaths of myrtle and ivy, and set off on an archaeological jaunt on Lake Garda. As they went they played a lute and addressed one another as Emperor and Consuls. At the end of the day they came to

> the temple [that is church] of the blessed Peter in Sermione, entered it and offered mighty praises with the deepest devotion to the High Thunderer and his glorious Mother, especially because he had illuminated their hearts to make up the party, opened their minds to seek and search out such noble places, granted them so many fine and pleasant sights and such speedy discovery of quite a few antiquities.
>
> From C. Mitchell, 'Archaeology and Romance', in *Italian Renaissance Studies*, ed. E. F. Jacob, Faber, 1960, p. 478.

> For their own enjoyment artists should associate with poets and orators who have many embellishments in common with painters and who have a broad knowledge of many things. These could be very useful in beautifully composing the *istoria* whose greatest praise consists in the invention. A beautiful invention has such force, as will be seen, that even without painting it is pleasing in itself alone. Invention is praised when one reads the description of Calumny which Lucian recounts was painted by Apelles. I do not think it alien to our subject. I will narrate it here in order to point out to painters where they ought to be most aware and careful in their inventions. In this painting there was a man with very large ears. Near him, on either side, stood two women, one called Ignorance, the other Suspicion. Farther, on the other side, came Calumny, a woman who appeared most beautiful but seemed too crafty in the face. In her right hand she held a lighted torch, with the other hand she dragged by the hair a young man who held up his arms to heaven. There was also a man, pale, ugly all filthy and with an iniquitous aspect, who could be compared to one who has become thin and feverish with long fatigues on the fields of battle; he was the guide of Calumny and was called Hatred. And there were two other women, serving women of Calumny who arranged her ornaments and robes. They were called Envy and Fraud. Behind these was Penitence, a woman dressed in funereal robes, who stood as if completely dejected. Behind her followed a young girl, shameful and modest, called Truth. If this story pleased as it was being told, think how much pleasure and delight there must have been in seeing it painted by the hand of Apelles.
>
> I should like to see those three sisters [The Three Graces] to whom Hesiod gave the names of Aglaia, Euphrosyne and Thalia, who were painted laughing and taking each other by the hand, with their clothes girdled and very clean. This symbolizes liberality, since one of these sisters gives, the other receives, the third returns the benefit; these degrees ought to be in all perfect liberality.
>
> Alberti, pp. 90–1.

In 1435 Alberti suggested two subjects, *The Three Graces* and *The Calumny of Apelles*, to artists. The text for the latter had been translated from Greek into Latin by the humanist Guarino da Verona in 1408. In 1485 Botticelli painted *A Calumny* (Units 5–6, Section 8.3). He was the first painter to do so.

In 1502 Raphael painted a version of *The Three Graces* (Figure 105). Compare his version with a medieval one (Figure 106) and a classical one (Figure 88) which he had certainly not seen. Raphael probably, modelled his group on the classical sculpture of the Graces now in Siena (Figure 107). Since it was broken, how far would that have helped him to recapture the classical poses?

He might have known Petrarch's description of the Three Graces too:

> The first one had her back turned to us, but the other two had their eyes and faces turned towards us. Their arms were interlaced in ties of exquisite whiteness.
>
> From *The Survival of the Pagan Gods*, J. Seznec, Harper, 1961, p. 134.

DISCUSSION

74 One important development for artists wanting to be 'classical' was the sort of co-operation between artists and humanists which could produce Mantegna's boat trip, or the Report, perhaps by Raphael on Ancient Rome for an antiquarian Pope. It was the sort of co-operation between artists, and poets, and intellectuals which Alberti had advised. But it was typical that this sort of co-operation (which could produce an erudite picture with classical subject matter like Botticelli's *Calumny*) did not occur until some time after Alberti's suggestion, for co-operation between artists and 'orators' or humanists, and many years after texts like Lucian were available, perhaps because artists lacked contact with humanists, but also because of two other factors. Classical models, once discovered, had of course to be assimilated into another media (usually from sculpture to painting) before they could be used with ease and seem more than quotations. It is true too, that classical art could only be assimilated and used 'naturally' when classicism lost the taint of evil or paganism which had prompted the citizens of Siena in the previous century to break up a classical statue of Venus. Artists had to stop feeling that classical art was 'pagan' and sensual. Alberti's and Feliciano's habit of calling God 'Summum Tonans' or 'the one who thunders on high', like Jupiter, is symptomatic of the way 'classical' and 'Christian' were coming to seem less separate. It was, you will remember, between the 1460s and 1490s in Florence that Ficino was synthesizing Platonism and Christianity, for the circle of poets and philosophers around the Medici (see Units 5–6, Section 5.0).

75 Now, throughout this section, I've been misleading in two ways. I've talked as though certain painters 'lacked' classical features, and as though there was some 'perfect' recreation of classicism with which all 'efforts' are compared. I've also genuinely found it very difficult to define what exactly can be attributed to classical influence. Do we recognize classical influence by recording certain specific motifs, ornaments, costumes or poses? Or in the vaguer and more important features like treatment of space, depth, action or mood? Where classicism is almost synonymous with 'realism' it is almost impossible to tell when an artist has observed for himself or 'copied'. I shall try to deal with this problem in the next section. What really happened was, probably, that artists reinterpreted classicism more or less as it suited their needs. Raphael didn't really paint the poets on Parnassus as a Roman painter would have done. He added Dante and Ariosto, who were Italian poets, to his classical group and he painted it in the same room as he painted *The Disputà* which depicts the doctrines of the Church, as a decoration for the Papal apartments (Figure 108).

76 This reinterpretation of classical art was a subtle and complex matter, as you must have guessed when you examined the texts and versions of *The Three Graces*. Raphael may have known Petrarch's and Alberti's descriptions and the Siena relief. But the Sienese relief was broken and therefore didn't specify where the arms should be placed. Petrarch set the *mood* of the group, but he says 'the first' figure had her back turned and only that the arms were 'linked'. Alberti said the Graces were *girdled*, clothed, laughing and clean. He added the medieval symbolism of the group: that the two Graces

who turn to the spectator and the one who turns her back, form a 'chain of liberality', giving back what has been received. This would be interpreted in the Christian sense of 'good works', being doubly repaid. Raphael somehow matched a classical version (Figure 88) he had never seen except, perhaps, that the hands of the two facing Graces 'should be' on the shoulders of the one who turns her back. And yet, he gave it a new moral emphasis, as Panofsky has pointed out. For he gives the Graces the Golden Apples of Hesperides, which had been the *rewards* of Virtue, from another classical myth. Perhaps there is a moral for us in this example too: that a certain type of Renaissance artist was capable of making a great deal out of a very little, in the way of 'sources'. It emphasizes too the very piecemeal nature of classical sources available to artists and the way in which they adapted Christian themes to classical forms.

Figure 108

PART 2   PROPOSITION (i)   THE PHENOMENA OF FLORENTINE PAINTING BETWEEN ABOUT 1300 AND 1580 IS BEST EXPLAINED AS THE DEVELOPMENT OF A NEW STYLE, BASED ON INTEREST IN REALISM

77   The fact is, that it is still very difficult to prove or to believe that a few sculptures, some coins and a great deal of second or third hand copies of classical originals could produce the sort of revolutionary conception of mass, depth and human drama present in the work of Giotto, Cavallini, Lorenzetti and their contemporaries. The painter Duccio was probably not in contact with classical art at all, but you only have to look at his famous *Maestà* (Figure 109) to see that his work is similar to that of Giotto. In fact, the painters of the early fourteenth century in Tuscany produced what can better be called 'a *new type* of realistic volume space and human action', than 'a *recreation* of classical narrative aims'. Or, perhaps it was because the painters of fourteenth- and fifteenth-century Tuscany adopted aims similar to those of classical art, that, they often adopted similar techniques.

78   You will remember that Alberti, in his book *On Painting* did not believe that the revival of talent in the early fifteenth century had anything to do with the rediscovery of classical models. In fact he stresses how very praiseworthy his favourite sculptors and painters were, because they had no models or teachers. Vasari too, realized that artists, especially painters, had not derived their skill in realism and narration from classicism. How did Vasari interpret the revolution in painting which he called the 'rebirth'? Read the following passages from his *Lives* and decide the answer to this question.

> One day Cimabue was on his way from Florence to Vespignano, where he had some business to attend to, when he came across Giotto who, while the sheep were grazing near by, was drawing one of them by scratching with a slightly pointed stone on a smooth clean piece of rock. And this was before he had received any instruction.
>
> Vasari, pp. 56–7.

> Painting enjoyed no better fortune in those days, except in so far as popular enthusiasm meant that it was more in demand and there were more painters than architects and sculptors, and therefore it made more definite progress. Thus the old Byzantine style was completely abandoned – the first steps being taken by Cimabue and followed by Giotto – and a new style took its place: I like to call this Giotto's own style, since it was discovered by him and his pupils and was then generally admired and imitated by everybody. In this style of painting the unbroken outline was rejected, as well as staring eyes, feet on tiptoe, sharp hands, absence of shadow, and other Byzantine absurdities; these gave way to graceful heads and delicate colouring.
>
> Vasari, p. 88.

Now read the description of the reception of Duccio's *Maestà* in *Holt*, pages 134–6. How might it support Vasari's interpretation?

Vasari said that painters began to paint realistically and that painting developed because it was in popular demand, as the enthusiastic procession accompanying the Duccio supports.

179   Why should realism – a new look at nature – be connected with *popular* enthusiasm, and was Vasari's interpretation right? In fact, research has tended to support Vasari's interpretation. Between the twelfth and fourteenth centuries, in Tuscany, there was an extraordinary coincidence. Tuscan wealth and the power of its towns grew immensely. Prosperity seems to have produced a new type of patron – a layman, confident and hard-headed in his business methods and politics, often intent on proving that he 'had arrived' by his artistic patronage. At the same time two new and very dynamic religious orders – the Franciscans and the Dominicans were set up. They created what can only be called a radical, democratizing revolution in religious attitudes. What sort of art would you expect businessmen influenced by a certain amount of religious democracy and evangelism to like? How might the foundation of two new religious orders, just when patrons were eager to commission work, affect the demand on painting? What sort of work would be popular?

Laymen are unlikely to want the sort of paintings which emphasize the exclusive power of the church in a remotely symbolic manner. They are likely to want paintings which stress the congregation's as well as the priest's communication with and understanding of sacred figures: which assist private and personal devotion. This trend, towards a more homely and down-to-earth relationship between man and God would also be stressed by an evangelizing religious movement who wanted to win over congregations and who, originally at least, wanted to close the gap between clergy and laity.

180   St. Francis (1182–1226) had refused to allow his followers to own property and had tried to break down the barriers between priest, monk and layman. He had disliked elaborate church building and had embraced poverty and manual labour, in an attempt to get back to the simplicity of the early church. The ideas of some of his followers were declared heretical and by 1300 the sort of church decoration and institutionalization of his order which would have shocked him, were well under way. The great Franciscan church of *S. Croce* in Florence was being built. The church dedicated to him in Assisi had been decorated by Cimabue and Giotto. By then the order did not 'own' but 'used' property held by the Pope. But the radical impact of the order was still strong. The legends of St. Francis emphasized an extremely intimate and emotional relationship with God. In sermons and paintings there was an evangelizing attempt to move the spectator or listener by describing sacred stories 'as they had happened' in every little realistic and touching detail.

181   Lay confraternities had grown up. These were associations of laymen usually headed by a Franciscan Friar, devoted to a saint or sacred figure, and they became important patrons in the Renaissance. More concretely the creation and institutionalization of these two new orders – (the Franciscans and Dominicans) in Tuscany brought an upsurge of church building; a tremendous demand for architectural and artistic patronage of all sorts. You probably remember that John Larner (Unit 7) described in his television programme how quickly the church of *S. Croce* with its many chapels was filled with murals commissioned by the newly established merchant aristocracy like the Bardi and Peruzzi. By and large then, historical research has reinforced Vasari's claim that the revolution in style was a response to popular demand: has 'filled out' his interpretation that artists 'turned to Nature', rather than to classical art.

Proposition (ii)   This development was not consistent throughout the period 1300–1520

82   But, as with the question of classical influence, we have to ask whether the trend away from symbolism towards narrative realism was consistently developed between the 1300s and the sixteenth century. How do you think the devastation of the Black Death and economic decline in Tuscany between about 1340 and 1400 might affect the function of art? Would patrons still feel confident about this world and the joys of living? Would congregations who thought the Black Death was 'a lesson' to sinners like themselves feel love, affection, and nearness to God?

Just as there seems to have been a hiatus in the development of interest in classical art during this period, so Meillard Meiss, in his book called *Painting in Florence and Siena after the Black Death* has shown that there was a similar break in the development of the trend in narrative realism. Intimate scenes were replaced by more diagrammatic compositions expressing the separateness and superiority of sacred figures. Symbolism often replaced narration: that is, compositions were organized again around beautiful but hierarchical patterns, and figures were related to one another according to their status in the universe, their moral worth or 'importance' rather than arranged more haphazardly according to the part they played in a human and touching story. Everywhere the authority of the church and the sufferings of sinners was stressed. The humane and confident mood of Giotto's art was denied. Look carefully at *The Madonna of Humility* by the workshop of Simone Martini, painted in the the 1330s and *The Madonna of Humility* by a follower of Nardo di Cione painted in the 1360s, and read this passage from Meiss' book (Figures 110, 111):

> The Madonna of Humility created in the second quarter of the century as an intimate image of the Virgin's sympathy and love, was so drastically transformed after 1350 as to lose much of its original meaning. Seated on a cushion, The Madonna is raised above the ground and suspended in an area of gold, becoming less the humble mother than an exalted celestial apparition – whereas the painters of the early Trecento [fourteenth century] brought the sacred figures down to earth literally and figuratively, those of the third quarter of the century projected them upward again.
>
> *Painting in Florence and Siena after the Black Death*, M. Meiss, 1951, Harper and Row, p. 41.

It looks then, as though the art of Giotto and his contemporaries was a proto-Renaissance. Neither interest in classical art, nor in the problems of narrative realism developed consistently between 1300 or so and the 1520s.

Proposition (iii)   Realism in art was related to the growth of a sense of intimacy between man and God

83   But what *exactly* has interest in telling a pictorial story to do with realism and the techniques of perspective, drawing from life, anatomy, portraiture and so on, associated with it? Why should the fact that artist and patron desired to express an intimate devotional relationship with sacred figures lead to the

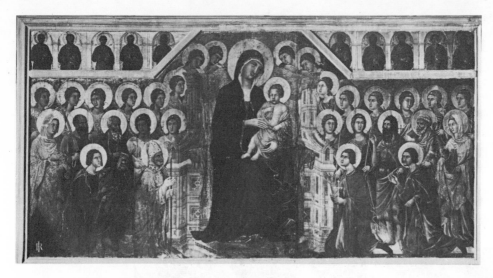

Figure 109

Figure 110

Figure 111

refinement of realism? Why should popular enthusiasm for art be associated with the discovery of scientific perspective or the dissolution of the 'surface' of the painting? Look back at my table of comparison between medieval art and classical art (paragraph 148). With the help of the following quotations, by Dominici, Alberti and Bonaventura, try to define the function of 'realism' in narrative 'evangelist' art and what sort of demands are made on it.

Dominici (1356–1419) was a Dominican with close associations with the church of *S. M. Novella* in Florence. He disliked the new humanist interest in pagan authors intensely, thinking it an enthusiasm for style rather than content in writing. In 1405 he advised on the religious education of children:

> The first thing is to have in the house paintings of holy boys and young virgins in which your child, while he is still in swaddling clothes can delight himself, since like calls to like with the deeds and characteristics which appeal to childhood . . . suitable themes

are the Virgin Mary with the Child on her arm and a little bird or pomegranate in his hand. A good motif would also be the suckling Christ, or Christ sleeping in his mother's lap. . . . Thus let the child mirror himself in the Holy Baptist dressed in a camel's skin.

Regola del Governo di Cura familiare, G. Dominici,
ed. D. Salvi, 1860, pp. 130ff.

Dominici goes on to say that pictures are 'the books of the simple' and to warn against pictures made of gold and precious stones for by these the young are made 'more idolatrous than believing'. Rather, the young child should see 'figures of reality'.

The *istoria* [narrative] which merits both praise and admiration will be so agreeably and pleasantly attractive that it will capture the eye of whatever learned or unlearned person is looking at it and will move his soul. That which first gives pleasure in the *istoria* comes from copiousness and variety of things . . . I say that *istoria* is most copious in which in their places are mixed old, young, maidens, women, youths, young boys, fowls, small dogs, birds, horses, sheep, buildings, landscapes and all similar things.

Alberti, p. 75

The *istoria* [narrative] will move the soul of the beholder when each man painted there clearly shows the movement of his own soul. It happens in nature that nothing more than herself is found capable of things like herself: we weep with the weeping, laugh with the laughing and grieve with the grieving. The movements of the soul are made known by the movements of the body. . . . Thus all the movements of the body should be closely observed by the painter. . . . Who could ever without the greatest study [of Nature] express faces in which mouth, chin, eyes, cheeks, forehead and eyebrows all were in harmony with laughter or weeping. For this reason it is best to learn them from nature. . . . The following demonstrates what the painter should seek out in nature. Where the face of some well known man is put in the *istoria* – even though there are other figures of a much more perfect art and more pleasing than this one – that well-known face will draw to itself all the eyes of those looking at the *istoria*. So great is the force of anything drawn from nature.

Alberti, pp. 77–8, 93–4.

In an *istoria* I like to see someone who admonishes and points out to us what is happening these; or beckons with his hand to see; or menaces with an angry face and with flashing eyes, so that no-one should come near; or shows some danger or marvellous thing there; or invites us to weep or to laugh together with them.

Alberti, p. 78.

Draw near, dear handmaiden, with loving feet to Jesus wounded, to Jesus crowned with thorns, to Jesus fastened on the gibbet of the cross, and be not content, as the blessed Apostle Thomas was, merely to see in his hands the point of the nails . . but rather go right in, through the opening in his side, to the very heart of Jesus where, transformed by the most burning love of Christ, held by the nails of Divine Love, pierced by the lance of profound Charity, and wounded by the sword of deep compassion, you will know no other wish or desire or hope of consolation except to die with Christ on the Cross, so that you can say with St. Paul: 'I am crucified with Christ. I live, yet not I but Christ liveth in me'.

A letter from Bonaventura to a Poor Clare,
from J. Moorman (1968) *The Franciscan Order*,
Oxford University Press, p. 260.

84 Alberti obviously feels that painting must capture the eye and make the onlookers want to linger over the delightful and varied details in a scene. The painting then, must catch the attention positively and induce it. It must also move the soul of the spectator. As Dominici stresses, the onlooker must see himself mirrored in the scene so that he can react in sympathy to the emotions represented in the figures. Each writer uses words like 'capture' 'move' 'catch'

'calls' to describe the way the painter must very actively grab and focus the attention of the spectator. For each, the means to this strong communication is realism. Only if the painter can represent figures under the impact of emotions or ideas which are recognizably similar to the spectator's own, can he really make him see himself *reflected* in the scene. Only if he is skilled enough in portraying the difficult emotions of weeping, laughter, anger and so on can he really make the spectator 'weep with the weeping, laugh with the laughing and grieve with the grieving'. To make the onlooker believe in the scene represented he has to be able to create tangible 'traversible' space and volume, enough like the real world to allow the spectator to enter into the scene emotionally, and, almost, physically. And it is only by an intensive and rigorous study of nature that the painter learns how to make a scene a mirror to the spectator: through perspective that he can make the spectator *share* the ground-level and space of figures in the picture. You will have noted too that the letter from Bonaventura to a Poor Clare lays tremendous emphasis on the way contemplation of Christ's human life, and entering into it in a most 'physical' way helps prayer. This type of contemplation was part of the Franciscan method of preaching and teaching. It lays great stress on the imaginative reconstruction of every little detail in a sacred scene. In a very real sense Renaissance religious paintings are meant to be sermons: even painted miracles for those with poor imaginations.

185   Telling a story, using realistic techniques and creating an intimate connection between spectator and sacred figures are inextricably involved. Once symbolism is even partially abandoned as a way of indicating the meaning of a painting, the figures themselves have to tell the story, direct to the spectator. Those figures, whether God, the Virgin or a human participant in the 'event', have to communicate their feelings in a way not too dissimilar to the spectator from that with which he recognizes 'what people feel' in his everyday life. They have to be *realistic*. Further they are bound to be more familiar to him, less super-natural and remote, than figures represented in a symbolic form, simply *because* he *must* understand them in everyday terms. We do not know whether telling a story using realism, or creating an intimate relationship between God and man, came first. But both these features are more or less interdependent. Telling a story in realistic terms involves skill in portraiture and in landscape. In fact these are innovations only remotely related to classical art. Fifteenth century painters probably knew that ancient painters had produced landscapes and portraits, but their interest in them seems to have been independent. There were landscape scenes and portraits amongst Giotto's contemporaries. Look for a moment at the landscape in Lorenzetti's *Good Government in the Country*; (Figure 93) but significantly it was really in the fifteenth century that both landscape and portraiture (to delight and arrest the spectator) became usual. Both the fact that landscape was not something artists could copy from antique sarcophagi, and the fact that Dominici was against the revival of classical style in literature but *for* the creation of *figures of reality*, should emphasize that interest in classicism and realism did not by any means always go hand in hand.

EXERCISE

186   Now I want you to examine Ghirlandaio's frescoes in the Sassetti Chapel in S. Trinità in Florence (Figures 112-13). They illustrate scenes from the life of St. Francis and they were painted between 1482 and 1486. Look at them in the light of what both Dominici and Alberti said about the function of painting. Then read the following evidence about the Chapel and decide (1) how it supports our thesis about the economic and social background to Florentine art, and (2) whether, on this evidence, you would interpret the 'naturalism', the 'humanization' and, in some cases the 'secularization' of religious art during this period as indicative of a *decrease* in religious enthusiasm or piety?

The topmost scene on the altar wall (Figure 112) shows St. Francis receiving confirmation of his Rule from the Pope, in the Piazza della Signoria (which is not, of course, where this event actually happened), with the Medici children and their tutor Poliziano (Units 5–6, Section 3.7) in the foreground coming up some stairs. In the centre is St. Francis resuscitating a boy of the Spini family (Figure 113). This family had been leading businessmen of twelfth-century Florence, as the Medici and Sassetti were of fifteenth-century Florence. In the background is a view over the bridge of *S. Trinità* and on the right is the façade of the church of *S. Trinità*, before it received its seventeenth-century façade. On either side of the altar are the kneeling figures of the donor Francesco Sassetti and his wife. Their bodies are in two classical sarcophagi on either side of the altar. The altar-piece represents the *Adoration* (*Murray*, Figure 225) complete with painted classical sarcophagus. An inscription refers to the legend that the sarcophagus of a Roman centurion served Christ as a cradle. All the scenes include numerous portraits of the Sassetti family. Look carefully at a preparatory drawing for the topmost scene on the altar wall (Figure 114). What differences are there between the drawing and the *fresco*? What do you conclude from these differences?

Figure 112

Figure 113

DISCUSSION

187   Both artist and patron (or one of the two) must have made a conscious decision to make portraiture of living notables prominent in the scenes, and to set them against contemporary townscapes of the political and business life of Florence, rather than in church settings. The drawing we possess doesn't in fact show the Medici children and their tutors very prominently, and it shows a church interior as background, rather than the final choice, of the Piazza della Signoria. The life of St. Francis is therefore represented as though it was part and parcel of Florentine social and political life, and part of Sassetti's life too. The Chapel can, in fact, be seen as a symbol of the intimate religious devotion which emphasizes the personal relationship between a Saint and a worshipper. It's typical, that in this chapel, as in Masaccio's *Trinity* (Plate 5) the two patrons are as big or bigger than the sacred figures.

188   In the light of Alberti's and Dominici's statements, the portraits, the landscapes, the introduction of street scenes, the varied figures and 'extraneous' incidents, are all part of the aim to delight, attract and move the spectator: to make him feel at home and very close to these moving and miraculous events. They should emphatically *not* be interpreted as secular adjuncts or even distractions from the religious story. The fact that Ghirlandaio placed St. Francis amongst contemporary figures in a busy street or the political centre of Florence is an indication of how strongly moved Sassetti and his friends must have been by a saint whose ideas still seemed very real to them, and how strongly Ghirlandaio wished the spectator to feel *like* the painted contemporary participants in these miraculous events.

189   In fact, between the thirteenth and fifteenth centuries there is a great deal of evidence that private, personal devotions increased, and changed in tone. Especially when printing got under way small devotional images (panel-paintings or little woodcuts) and private prayer books were produced. These private devotional images often consisted of groups of well-loved sacred figures extracted, as it were, from larger narrative scenes (*Murray*, Figures 152–5). The sacred figure is often treated as an intimate portrait so that Christ or the Virgin present the invitation to close contact for the worshipper, no longer occupied with some complex story of their own or in propagating Church dogma in symbolic fashion (*Murray*, Figure 73). In public painting too, the emphasis was on choosing subjects which would give an opportunity to show homely detail, like *The Nativity*, or passionate emotions like the scenes from *The Passion*. Rather than illustrating the New or Old Testament, artists represented all sorts of legends surrounding the lives of their favourite saints or the relatives of the Virgin Mary. A typical example of this is *The Legend of the True Cross*, which was the subject of many paintings including the frescoes at Arezzo by Piero della Francesca (*Murray*, Figure 100).

190   The most important single pictorial discovery, which really emphasizes how independent Florentine painting was from classical art, was the invention of scientific perspective by Brunelleschi in the 1420s.

> How difficult [perspective] is can be seen in the work of antique sculptors and painters; perhaps because it was obscure it was hidden and unknown to them. One scarcely sees a single antique [narrative] aptly composed.
> Alberti, p. 58.

I shall not repeat the technical description of Brunelleschi's and Alberti's perspective, so you should re-read the summary in Appendix I, Unit 8, at this point. Then compare these paintings: *The Resuscitation of a Child of the Spini Family* by Ghirlandaio (Figure 113) and *The Expulsion of the Traders from the Temple* by Giotto (Plate 3). You should apply perspective diagrams to both paintings, deciding whether and where their vanishing point exists and deciding how their respective types of perspective affect their design and the spectator. Does scientific perspective enable the artist to tell a story and affect the spectator more easily?

DISCUSSION

191   The viewing point of the spectator on to these two scenes varies tremendously. In Ghirlandaio's picture there is a single vanishing point located on or rather 'behind' the child's bed. This point is the height of the spectator's eye, so he is actually looking at the scene on the level of the participants. The perspective therefore plainly indicates where the spectator must be standing. It focuses on him. This focus emphasizes the way perspective reinforced the function of a painting as an appeal to an individual. It's easy to see too that perspective depth – the structure of lines leading to a central point in depth – also provided the painter with the formal means to *pull* the spectator deep into the picture space, as well as allowing the painter to place more figures and incidents at varying depths in space, rather than having to place them all at the front. Perspective therefore allows the painter to handle more figures, more coherently. Note too that there is no feeling that the building stops where it meets the picture surface, as in *The Expulsion* with its doll's house view. The wall has become a window, or better, a door through into the scene. Perspective too, in Ghirlandaio's picture is in fact much more than a way of setting up a depth situation. It actually creates a new type of symbolism. For the vanishing point lies behind the child's bed and emphasizes his importance in the painting.

192   *The Expulsion* has no single vanishing point. This was impossible without Alberti's construction. Consequently the scene lacks focus and fails to specify or require the presence of a spectator at any particular point. Pattern, reinforcing the spectator's awareness of the surface wall is very strong. There is a strong sense of receding space, in the indications of the building but the figures are all on the front plane and they move across the space – not towards or away from the spectator. Still, as John White has so strongly emphasized in his book *The Birth and Rebirth of Pictorial Space* it is quite wrong to see Brunelleschi's discovery as an innovation pure and simple. Unless Giotto and his contemporaries had begun to break down the surface patterns of the painted wall, and attempted to focus the spectators gaze and lead his eye into depth, Brunelleschi's rationalization of these aims, would hardly have been possible.

193   One other important way in which the narrative aim seems to have driven artists to re-examine 'reality' was an increasing interest in anatomy. There is little evidence of sustained interest in anatomy amongst fourteenth century or classical artists, but in the fifteenth century there were many artists—Pollaiuolo, Leonardo, Michelangelo, and Signorelli—who all seem to have studied the structure of the human body intensively (*Murray*, Figures 160, 216). Typically it was Alberti who first urged the study of anatomy on painters and justified his interest:

> We ought to have a certain rule for the size of the members. In this measuring it would be useful to isolate each bone of the animal, on this add its muscles, then clothe all of it with its flesh. Here someone will object that I have said above that the painter has only to do with things which are visible. He has a good memory. Before dressing a man we first draw him nude, then we enfold him in draperies. So in painting the nude we place first his bones and muscles which we then cover with flesh so that it is

not difficult to understand where each muscle is beneath. Since nature has here carried the measurements to a mean, there is not a little utility in recognizing them. Serious painters will take this task on themselves from nature. They will put as much study and work into remembering what they take from nature as they do in discovering it. A thing to remember: to measure an animate body take one of its members by which the others can be measured. Vitruvius, the architect, measured the height of man by the feet. It seems a more worthy thing to me for the other members to have reference to the head, because I have noticed as common in all men that the foot is as long as from the chin to the crown of the head. Thus one member is taken which corresponds to all the other members in such a way that none of them is non-proportional to the others in length and width.

Alberti, p. 73.

You should note that anatomy is spoken of in close association with proportion, and the study of anatomy may be not only motivated by a thoroughgoing interest in realistic accuracy, but also relate to the need to wipe out all tendencies to 'Gothic' proportions in figures by 'going back to the beginning'. It is therefore indirectly linked to interest in classical art.

194   I have said that interest in realism was often connected with interest in classical style, either because both realism and classicism seemed to represent a new style, or because classical styles could teach realistic techniques. But was this a general rule? Look at Ghirlandaio's *Adoration* for the Sassetti chapel (*Murray*, Figure 225) and at Hugo Van der Goes *Adoration* which was a precious possession of the Florentine banking family, the Portinari (*Murray*, Figure 131). What are your conclusions?

Figure 114

Ghirlandaio has, in fact, 'lifted' Van der Goes' shepherds and put them into his own picture. It is interesting too, that Florentine patrons were not by any means exclusively interested in their own artists' classicism, but liked Flemish painting and tapestry too. Van Eyck's special technique of oil painting with its smooth and subtle effects, as well as the painstaking Flemish treatment of portraiture and landscape, was a major influence on Florentine art of the fifteenth century. So there was no such thing as a straight, artistic *clash* between Northern and Italian art, or between 'classical' and 'medieval'.

195   Interest in landscape, portraiture, narration, perspective and anatomy are all symptomatic of an interest in realism. But was holding up a mirror to Nature the only aim of these artists? In the final part of this unit I want to examine three main ways in which the function of paintings and the difficulties and drawbacks of the 'techniques of realism' modified the ability or desire of Florentine artists to copy what they saw.

Proposition (iv)   For Renaissance painters realism did not mean painting what they saw

(a)   *Fidelity to Nature versus tradition and the problems of creating a 'slice of life'*

196   First of all, read this passage from Alberti's *On Painting*, and look again at his description of the importance of anatomy. Is Alberti thinking of a painter who sets up his canvas, panel or whatever in front of a group of objects and figures and produces a replica of what he sees?

> Youths who first come to painting . . . should learn each distinct form of each member and commit to memory whatever differences there may be in each member. . . . You will see some whose nose projects and is humped, others will have flaring simian nostrils, others pendant lips, still others the adornment of thin lips. . . . Again he should note that our youthful members, as can be seen, are round and delicate as if turned: in a more tried age they are harsh and angular. All these things the studious painter will know from nature. . . . He will continually be wide awake with his eyes and mind in this investigation.
>
> Alberti, p. 92.

Given that perspective realism depends on looking at a picture from one point and with one eye closed, is this the normal way of looking at things and do you think that is the way spectators looked at these paintings? Look at Pollaiuolo's *Martyrdom of San Sebastian* (Plate 9) and at *The Flood* by Paolo Uccello (Figure 115). Are these representations of 'a slice of life' and do realistic 'techniques' always produce realistic effects?

If, as an artist, you are asked to paint several scenes on the walls of a chapel can you possibly make the wall into 'a window'? Look at the paintings in Ghirlandaio's Sassetti Chapel (Figures 112-13). Note down your answers to these questions before reading on.

DISCUSSION

97   Now, it is true that Dominici said the spectator must see himself *mirrored* in the picture, and that Alberti and subsequent artists *did* obviously attempt to remain 'wide-awake' continually to the world around them. Observing the expressions of people, investigating the structure of the body, painting portraits of people and landscapes, creating mathematical laws which will counterfeit visual experience, are all symptoms of a moving and rigorous attempt to take a new look at the visual world. But, ultimately, these artists observed in order to *codify*. They couldn't really do anything else given the bewildering variety of

visual experience, and the fact (of which Alberti was very aware) that there are many visual effects the painter *wants* to capture but cannot actually see because of their speed or subtlety. It is this sort of codification which is behind the scientific aspect of Florentine 'naturalism'. Artists did not look at a scene or a figure and perspectivize or 'anatomize' it. They constructed a scene or a figure built up from all their knowledge of perspective and anatomy and made it look real. Artists couldn't look afresh at every problem. Their lives were bound up in a workshop tradition which gave them work and taught them those short-cuts to 'realism' which could never have been discovered or modified afresh by each artist. In a sense it was the very rigorousness involved in learning realistic techniques which meant that artists had to retain the conventions of past generations. Anyway, to create the type of complex compositions which Renaissance artists and patrons admired, you would need to get people to pose for days, and to be actors so that they could 'reproduce' the emotions you wanted. You would need to paint straight onto the canvas or wall. You wouldn't be able to afford plants which withered or changes of weather. These are universal problems in painting 'a slice of life' or 'mirroring what you see'. But it must be obvious that it is easier to compromise; to build up a visual memory of 'what people look like when they shout', or walk or do anything you might want to represent, and record your ideas on paper so that you can copy and recombine them; that it is easier to copy other people's drawings, or make little wood or clay models which you can then drape or move into any position you want. When artists did use human models they used them in rather unrealistic ways. For instance, in Pollaiuolo's *Martyrdom of Sebastian* (Plate 9), the artist has obviously used a human model for the four archers in the foreground, but he only used the *one* model, and attempted to disguise it by altering the postures of the figures. They are the same figure painted four times.

198   You will have realized too that Brunelleschi's perspective does not reproduce reality so much as create 'a pictorial reality', which, while it's good enough for the purpose of creating a 'window' effect, doesn't really counterfeit the realities of binocular vision or the way our eyes move and refocus continually as we scan a scene. Over and above this, realistic techniques like perspective and anatomy could become so much a matter of the display of skill, that they negated the effects intended. Look for a moment at Uccello's *Flood* (Figure 115) and at Pollaiuolo's *Hercules and the Hydra* (Figure 104). Perhaps because both perspective and anatomy are close to scientific description or diagram, an artist who is fasci- nated by them tends to emphasize linear pattern, chopping up the surface of the canvas, or a figure. Finally, a painter who has to represent several scenes on a wall cannot easily elide the wall. He can only create several 'windows' on the wall. You will find, in Unit 13 (Part 2(iii)(a)) that Leonardo criticized this compartmentalization of the wall, but few painters ever did treat one wall as one enormous scene.

(b)   *Fidelity to Nature and teaching the illiterate*

199   Now I want you to read St. Gregory's description of the function of art and examine two paintings and their subject matter. Then decide how the didactic function of religious art delimits the use of 'naturalism' in painting, and suggest how the revolutionary discoveries in 'how to make things look real' might help the artist to express certain religious ideas – especially the 'supernatural'.

> What the scripture teaches those who read, this same the image shows to those who cannot read, but see; because in it, even the ignorant see whom they ought to follow. In the image those who do not know letters are able to read.
>
> St. Gregory, *Letter to Serenus, The Rise of the Dramatic Close-up in fifteenth-century Devotional Painting*, S. Ringbom, 1965, p. 11.

Look carefully at *The Apotheosis of St. Thomas Aquinas* (Figure 116) by Andrea da Firenze and *The Disputà* (Figure 108) by Raphael. St. Thomas is shown triumphant amongst the true and false advocates of the Lord. *The Disputà* is a visible representation of the Christian Faith. In heaven the Trinity and saints, apostles and prophets: on earth the participation of mankind in the Divine Presence through the mystery of the Eucharist.

DISCUSSION

200 It must be obvoius that it is *very* easy to paint 'realistically' if you only have to paint a landscape or a portrait, but virtually impossible if you wish to explain ideas or metaphysical and spiritual relationships. Raphael possesses more skill than Andrea in naturalism. He can define the position of figures in space more closely. He can paint a delicate landscape, counterfeit clouds and draw perspective. But, in that he has to present complex ideas and define 'who' all his figures are, like Andrea da Firenze, and even like the artist who painted *The Entry into Jerusalem* (Figure 90), he has to use a diagrammatic composition and he has to use symbols of an explicit sort. It is not possible to express the doctrine of the Church in terms of narrative drama alone. And that is why Andrea's and Raphael's pictures look very similar. Both depend on symbolism of place – up for God, down for man – and on the sort of conventional, even 'dictionary' symbolism, dictating, for instance, that St. Peter holds keys. The dilemma of all Renaissance painting was that it had to try to express the spiritual – the other-wordly – and *ideas* in terms of naturalism. Interestingly enough though, once spectators expect 'realism' in a painting, they can be 'informed' that some event or figure *is* divine by a partial or entire suspension of realism. Note in Raphael's picture the *mandorla* or golden halo of rays surrounding Christ and the Dove. Look too at Masaccio's *Trinity* (Plate 5) and at Ghirlandaio's *St. Francis resuscitating a child of the Spini Family* (Figure 113). How has divinity been symbolized?

Figure 115

201   Ghirlandaio's picture signifies St. Francis' holiness by surrounding him in a nimbus of clouds, cut off from the everyday world. Masaccio symbolizes the *Trinity* by *not* foreshortening either the figure of Christ or God and making the position of the Cross within the arch very difficult to place. Masaccio has also *used* the perspective 'diagram' which the onlooker is 'aware of' beneath the structure of the picture to set the Trinity apart, for the vanishing point of the scene is beneath the foot of the cross and encloses the Trinity in an upturned triangle of 'rays'. In other words, 'realism' was limited by the need for pictures to represent spirituality and ideas. But it also set up a symbolic system of its own: where perspective realism could be denied to represent the other-wordly, or where it could be used to emphasize the importance of a figure or idea.

(c)   *Fidelity to Nature and an Ideal of Beauty*

202   Again, I want you to examine some texts and pictures, this time asking how far and why Florentine painters' belief in their creativity and the need to produce beautiful and graceful pictures, conflicted with copying what they saw. The first text comes from *Four Dialogues on Painting* by Francesco Hollanda, purporting to represent conversations with Michelangelo and first published in 1549. Michelangelo had been asked to say why Italian painting is better than Flemish painting:

> In Flanders, they paint with a view to external exactness. They paint stuffs and masonry, the green grass of the fields, the shadow of the trees, and rivers and bridges, which they call landscapes, with many figures on this side and on that. And all this, though it pleases some persons, is done without reason or art, without symmetry or proportion, without skilful choice or boldness, and finally, without substance or vigour. . . . For good painting is nothing but a copy of the perfections of God, and a recollection of His painting; it is a music, and a melody which only the intellect can understand and that with great difficulty.
>
> *Four Dialogues on Painting*, F. Hollanda, trans. A. F. G. Bell, 1928, Oxford University Press p. 16.

> I shall define Beauty to be a harmony of all the parts in whatsoever subject it appears, fitted together with such proportion and connection that nothing could be added, diminished or altered, but for the worse.
>
> *The Ten Books on Architecture* L. B. Alberti, ed. J. Rykwert, 1965, Tiranti.

The following four quotations come from *On Painting* by Alberti:

> I dislike solitude in *istorie* [narratives], nevertheless I do not at all praise that copiousness which shrinks from dignity. I strongly approve in an *istoria* that which I see observed by tragic and comic poets. They tell a story with as few characters as possible. In my judgement no picture will be filled with so great a variety of things that nine or ten men are not able to act with dignity. I think pertinent to this the statement of Varro who admitted no more than nine guests to a banquet in order to avoid confusion.
>
> Alberti, p. 76.

> In every *istoria* variety is always pleasant. A painting in which there are bodies in many dissimilar poses is always especially pleasing. There some stand erect, planted on one foot, and show all the face with the hand high and the fingers joyous. In others the face is turned, the arms folded and the feet joined. And thus to each one is given his own action and flection of members; some are seated, others on one knee, others lying. If it is allowed here, there ought to be some nude and others part nude and part clothed in the painting; but always make use of shame and modesty. The parts of the body ugly to see and in the same way others which give little pleasure should be covered with draperies, with a few fronds or the hand. The ancients painted the portrait of Antigonos only from the part of the face where the eye was not lacking. It is said that Pericles' head was long and ugly, for this reason he – unlike others – was portrayed by

painters and sculptors wearing a helmet. Plutarch says that when the ancient painters depicted the kings, if there were some flaw in them which they did not wish to leave unnoticed, they 'corrected' it as much as they could while still keeping a likeness.
                                                                    Alberti, pp. 76–7.

In order to make a painting which the citizens placed in the temple of Lucina near Croton, Zeuxis, the most excellent and most skilled painter of all, did not rely rashly on his own skills as every painter does today. He thought that he would not be able to find so much beauty as he was looking for in a single body, since it was not given to a single one by nature. He chose, therefore, the five most beautiful young girls from the youth of that land in order to draw from them whatever beauty is praised in a woman. He was a wise painter.
                                                                    Alberti, p. 93.

A face which has its planes here large and there small, here raised and there depressed – similar to the faces of old women – would be most ugly in appearance. Those faces which have the planes joined in such a way that they take shades and lights agreeably and pleasantly, and have no harshness of the relief angles, these we should certainly say are beautiful and delicate faces.
                                                                    Alberti, p. 72.

Look at Masaccio's *Trinity* (Plate 5), Pollaiuolo's *Martyrdom of San Sebastian* (Plate 9) and at Uccello's *Attempt to destroy the Host* (Figure 117). Look out for geometrical patterns in the detail and the overall design in these paintings. Why are such 'symmetries' present? You should also examine a portrait of *Federigo da Montefeltro and his son* by Piero della Francesca (*Murray*, Figure 105). Federigo had lost his right eye.

Figure 116 (detail)

DISCUSSION

203   Michelangelo's insistence on symmetry, proportion and the intellectual nature of art reflects the theory that beauty derives its power from the way it mirrors the mathematical harmonies of the universe. It is a statement that painting, like architecture, has rhythms and ratios like music. One must not paint 'disproportionate' figures or construct 'imbalanced' scenes (although these are part of the visual world). Rather, compositions and figures must be 'tied together' in a 'harmonious' relation. This is why Masaccio's *Trinity* is a design

based on a triangle which is topped by God and holds the two patron's at its base, the cross on which Christ hangs, and the huge rectangular which contains the whole. It is why Pollaiuolo's *Martyrdom of San Sebastian* presents a central group which is really a triangle above a tipped circle, and why you will find that the room in Uccello's *Attempt to destroy the Host* is a square, while the scene 'outside' is half a square. Figures too were constructed on the Vitruvian proportions which Alberti describes. Such 'designs' often have little to do with the creation of perspective depth or pictorial 'reality', because you will notice, the compositional designs I've mentioned actually depend on treating the wall or canvas in two dimensions, as a pattern which continually pulls attention away from the idea that the painting is a 'window'.

Figures 116 and 117

04   These ideas are both highly Platonic and highly religious. The picture must be a copy of the perfections of God, of a higher Reality, not of the everyday world. In fact, Florentine painters wanted to create a new and better-than-natural pictorial Reality. The truly creative artist, they felt, was like a little god, selecting, modifying and refining to reconstruct the perfection of the world God would have been able to create but for the Fall of Man and the corruption of the sublunary world. So, 'correcting' or not showing the defects of a person whose portrait you were painting, or choosing various features and reconstructing them into a beautiful face, took on a very *moral* tone. Graceful faces, modelled in soft gradations of light and shade rather than 'old' ugly faces, represented an aspiration towards a moral as well as a physical ideal. Federigo da Montefeltre's portrait could therefore be felt to be *true* to his character.

05   The emphasis on the scientific and intellectual aspects of an artist's work and on his divine mission are, of course, related to the increasing demand for artistic status. I shall deal with these claims in Unit 12 on *Artistic Status*. Here I should add that the emphasis on 'symmetry' and 'selection' as an imitation of God, is perhaps also a 'rationalization' of the fact that 'symmetry' and 'selection' were forced upon artists. Symmetry in general design is part of the tradition of medieval design in painting. Both Renaissance and medieval paintings were dependent on the symbolism of 'up' for the heavenly, 'down' for hell or the world, 'centre' for importance, 'peripheral' for less important. This symbolism depends on place 'on' *not* 'beyond' a wall or canvas. It acts against the creation of pictorial depth. It should be emphasized though, that Brunelleschi's centralized vanishing point to which *all* shapes and dimensions in a painting are subsumed was a powerful *new* unifying force in a painting or sculpted relief: a design 'shape' which imprints itself on every painting after the 1430s. 'Michelangelo's' grand statement is also, after all, a glorification of the fact that selection was a practical necessity for the artist. Finally, as Alberti realized, there must be a balance between, say, variety and simplicity in a painting. Too many figures confuse comprehension of a scene. 'Too few' or 'too little' are both statements which *guide* the artist in his selection and composition; which help him sift and choose from what he sees around him. All in all, a painting like Botticelli's *Spring* (*Murray*, Figure 1), is not 'a slice of life'. It is only 'more realistic' than a medieval painting. Otherwise it is as 'naturalistic' a picture as any painting could be, which is graceful, delightful, decorative, harmonious and which communicates a complicated, intellectual, Platonic allegory.

06   The style of painting and sculpture at this time was certainly the product of a complex pattern of factors. Its chief characteristics seem to be a fascination with classical art (but often in a rather bastardized form), interest in certain types of realism (insofar as the ideological function of art permitted this) and a conviction that the artist should work scientifically and rationally. Very often there are conflicts between these ideals, and, of course, you could argue quite successfully that technical innovations like *fresco*, the bow-drill, oil-painting or bronze founding, were the salient factors in this new style. It is important too to stress that old habits died hard. We know, for instance, that sixteenth-century Florentine houses were often still full of those icons in the Byzantine manner which Dominici had criticized a hundred years earlier. Nor was the Renaissance the only one. It was just much more influential than previous ones.

RENAISSANCE AND REFORMATION

Historical Introduction

$\left.\begin{matrix} 1 \\ 2 \end{matrix}\right\}$ The Period and Its Significance

Economic and Social Developments

$\left.\begin{matrix} 3 \\ 4 \end{matrix}\right\}$ Economy and Society in Western Europe / The Transition from Feudalism to Capitalism

$\left.\begin{matrix} 5 \\ 6 \end{matrix}\right\}$ The Mediaeval Inheritance and the Revival of Classical Learning

Florence

7   Florentine Society 1382–1494

$\left.\begin{matrix} 8 \\ 9 \\ 10 \end{matrix}\right\}$ Sculpture 1400–70 / Architecture: Brunelleschi and Alberti 1400–72 / Painting 1300–1520

$\left.\begin{matrix} 11 \\ 12 \\ 13 \end{matrix}\right\}$ Iconography / Artistic Status / Leonardo

14   Machiavelli: *The Prince* and its Historical Context

Copernicus

$\left.\begin{matrix} 15 \\ 16 \end{matrix}\right\}$ The Background to Copernicus / The Copernican Revolution

Renaissance Music

$\left.\begin{matrix} 17 \\ 18 \\ 19 \end{matrix}\right\}$ Renaissance Music Part 1 / Renaissance Music Part 2 / Renaissance Music Part 3

The Reformation

$\left.\begin{matrix} 20 \\ 21 \end{matrix}\right\}$ Origins of the Reformation

$\left.\begin{matrix} 22 \\ 23 \end{matrix}\right\}$ Luther and Lutheranism

$\left.\begin{matrix} 24 \\ 25 \end{matrix}\right\}$ Calvin and Other Reformers

$\left.\begin{matrix} 26 \\ 27 \end{matrix}\right\}$ The Catholic Reformation

English Renaissance Literature

28   An Introduction to Elizabethan England

$\left.\begin{matrix} 29 \\ 30 \end{matrix}\right\}$ Elizabethan Poetry

$\left.\begin{matrix} 31 \\ 32 \end{matrix}\right\}$ Elizabethan and Jacobean Drama / *Doctor Faustus, The Changeling, The Alchemist*

$\left.\begin{matrix} 33 \\ 34 \end{matrix}\right\}$ *King Lear*

Plate 1

Plate 2

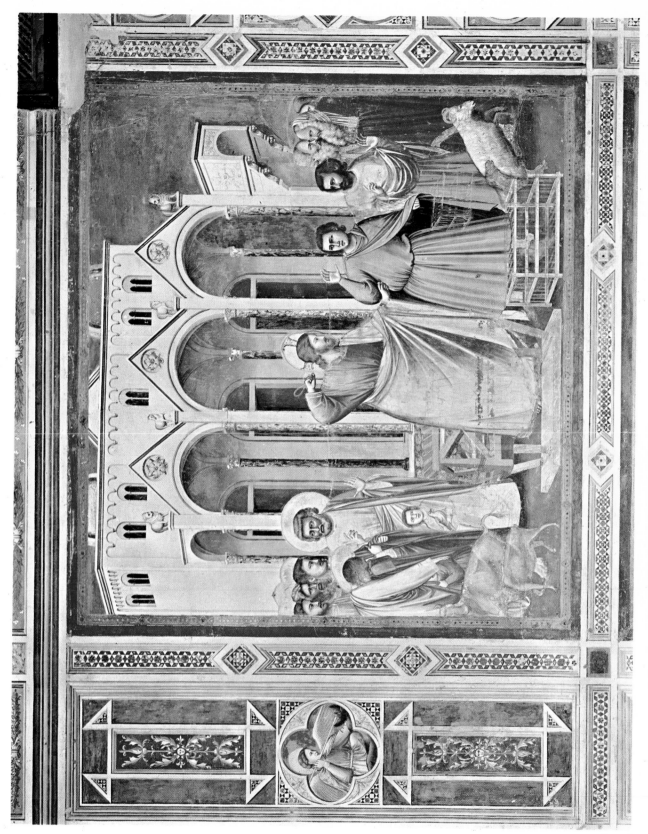

Plate 3

Plate 4

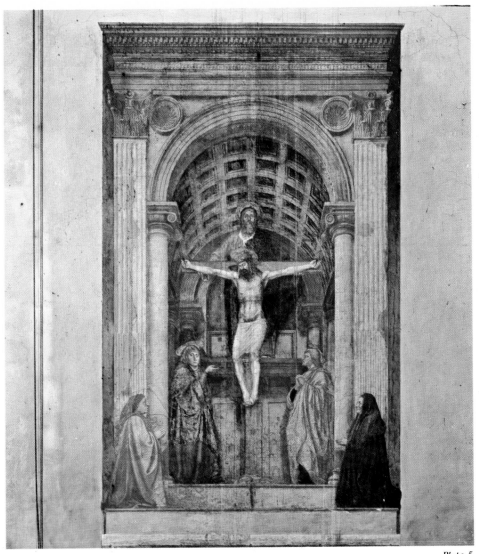

Plate 5

Plate 6

Plate 7

Plate 8

Plate 9